THE
MAYO
LOVER'S
COOKBOOK

HarperCollins*Publishers*
1 London Bridge Street
London SE1 9GF

www.harpercollins.co.uk

HarperCollins*Publishers*
Macken House, 39/40 Mayor Street Upper
Dublin 1, D01 C9W8, Ireland

First published by HarperCollins*Publishers* 2023

10 9 8 7 6 5 4 3 2 1

A catalogue record of this book is available from the British Library

ISBN 978-0-00-860751-7

Recipes: Heather Thomas
Photography: Sophie Fox
Food Styling: Pippa Leon
Prop Styling: Faye Wears

Printed in Latvia

WHEN USING KITCHEN APPLIANCES PLEASE ALWAYS FOLLOW
THE MANUFACTURER'S INSTRUCTIONS

THE
MAYO
LOVER'S
COOKBOOK

HEATHER THOMAS

HarperCollins*Publishers*

CONTENTS

INTRODUCTION

MAYONNAISE, OR MAYO, AS IT IS MOST AFFECTIONATELY KNOWN BY DEDICATED MAYONNAISE LOVERS, IS ONE OF THE WORLD'S MOST POPULAR SAUCES. THE GLOBAL MAYONNAISE MARKET IS VALUED AT A STAGGERING £10 BILLION, AND NEARLY EVERY COUNTRY HAS ITS OWN TAKE ON THIS CLASSIC SAUCE. DELICIOUSLY SMOOTH AND CREAMY, MAYONNAISE IS INCREDIBLY VERSATILE AND CAN BE USED AS A CONDIMENT, A SALAD DRESSING, A DIP, A SANDWICH FILLING, OR AS THE ESSENTIAL INGREDIENT IN SOME TRADITIONAL SAUCES, INCLUDING SAUCE TARTARE, AIOLI, ROUILLE AND REMOULADE.

HISTORY AND ORIGINS

The history of mayonnaise is shrouded in mystery and there is an ongoing dispute as to whether it originated in France or Spain. Some food historians trace its development back to the traditional French remoulade and aioli sauces and argue that the name is derived from the old French words for an egg yolk (*moyen*) and the verb 'to beat' (*mailler*).

However, it seems more likely that the first mayonnaise sauce was prepared in 1756 as part of a celebration feast in Mahon for the Duc de Richelieu after the French defeated the British fleet at the naval battle of Menorca in the Balearic Islands. Having no cream, his chef combined eggs with local olive oil to make a sauce and this became known as *mahonnaise*.

In the nineteenth century, mayonnaise became a popular sauce in European countries. However, it didn't take off in the United States until the early twentieth century when Richard Hellmann, a German immigrant, opened a delicatessen in New York. His customers liked the homemade mayonnaise dressing on his salads so much that he started producing it commercially and now Hellmann's mayonnaise is one of the world's best-known and favourite brands.

WHAT IS MAYONNAISE?

Traditional mayonnaise is made by beating oil, egg yolks and vinegar or lemon juice until they combine and emulsify into a thick, creamy sauce. A variety of ingredients can be added to enhance the flavour, colour and aroma, including mustard, herbs and spices. Supermarkets and delis now stock a wide range of commercially produced mayonnaise products, including light, extra light, vegan (eggless), Dijonnaise, baconnaise, and BBQ, lemon, garlic, chilli, katsu and truffle flavoured mayos.

MAKING MAYONNAISE

Homemade mayonnaise invariably tastes better than shop-bought. It's quick and easy to make and if you don't want to make it in the time-honoured way by beating with a balloon whisk, you can use a stick blender, hand-held electric whisk or a blender or food processor.

What you need

- **Oil**: use a lightly-flavoured or bland oil, which will not overpower the mayonnaise. Try groundnut (peanut), avocado, sunflower or a very light olive oil. Strongly flavoured extra-virgin olive oil is not recommended and seldom used.
- **Egg yolks**: use free-range organic egg yolks for the best flavour.
- **Acid (vinegar or lemon juice)**: choose from white or red wine or apple cider vinegar, or use fresh zesty lemon or lime juice.

GOLDEN RULES

Remember that mayonnaise is an emulsion and it's made by adding one ingredient (oil) very slowly, initially drop by drop, to another (egg yolks) until they combine and emulsify into a thick and creamy mixture. For the best results follow the guidelines below.

1. Make sure all the ingredients are at room temperature before you start. Don't use eggs straight from the fridge.
2. Add the oil one drop at a time, whisking well between each addition, until it starts to emulsify, and then add the rest of the oil slowly in a thin and steady trickle, beating all the time.
3. Don't worry if the mayonnaise splits and curdles – you can rescue it. Try one of the following remedies:
   - beat an egg yolk in a clean bowl and then beat in the curdled mayonnaise;
   - put 1 teaspoon of Dijon mustard into a clean bowl and gradually beat in the curdled mayonnaise a little at a time, until it comes together and emulsifies.

FLAVOURINGS

We have lots of exciting ideas for flavourings in the recipes in this book, including spicy ones such as guacamole, sriracha, sweet chilli and satay sauces and harissa; fresh-tasting ones such as lemon, mango and tzatziki; and savoury ones with truffles, feta cheese, blue cheese, pesto sauce, saffron, wasabi, miso and ouzo.

VEGAN MAYONNAISE

You can make delicious vegan mayo at home by substituting aquafaba (the drained liquid from tinned chickpeas) for the usual egg yolks (see page 13).

STORING MAYONNAISE

Homemade mayo, made with fresh egg yolks, can be stored in a sealed container in the fridge for two days. Jars of commercially made mayonnaise, once opened, will keep well in the fridge for up to two months.

CAUTION!

Babies and young children, pregnant women and elderly people should not eat mayonnaise made with raw, unpasteurized egg yolks, as it may contain salmonella bacteria. Most commercially produced mayonnaise brands use pasteurized eggs.

BAKING WITH MAYONNAISE

Strange as it seems, you can add mayonnaise to cakes, muffins, cookies, loaves and even breakfast pancakes to make them deliciously moist. It is sometimes used as a substitute for butter and/or eggs. Try the simple recipes in the baking section at the end of the book and see for yourself how well it works.

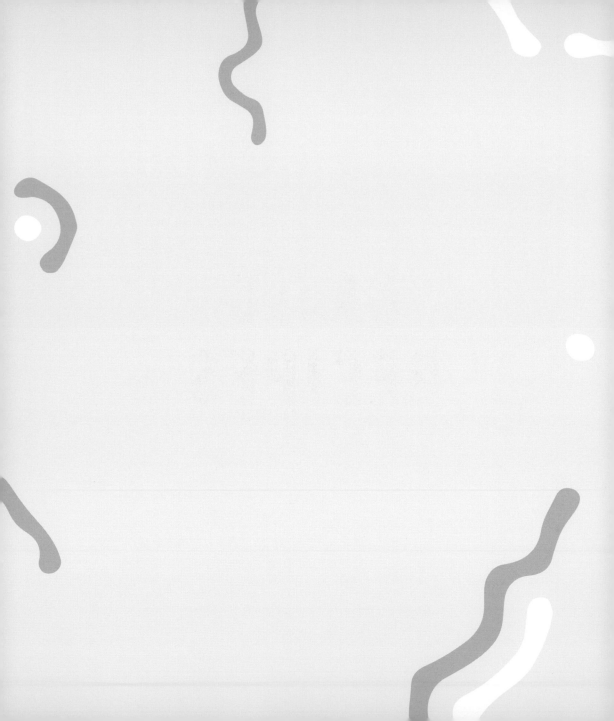

BASIC RECIPES

HOMEMADE MAYONNAISE

MAKES ABOUT 350ML/
12FL OZ (1½ CUPS)
PREP: 10 MINUTES

3 medium free-range egg yolks

1 tsp lemon juice or white wine
vinegar

1 tsp mild Dijon mustard (optional)

300ml/½ pint (1¼ cups) light
olive oil

sea salt and freshly ground
black pepper

VARIATIONS

- Use sunflower oil or rapeseed oil instead of olive oil.
- You can also make the mayo in an electric blender or using a stick blender.

THIS IS THE CLASSIC RECIPE FOR MAKING MAYONNAISE. IT'S A SIMPLE EMULSION OF LIGHT OLIVE OIL, EGG YOLKS, LEMON JUICE OR WHITE WINE VINEGAR AND MUSTARD (OPTIONAL). MANY PEOPLE WORRY ABOUT THE SAUCE CURDLING BUT IF YOU FOLLOW THE INSTRUCTIONS BELOW TO THE LETTER, YOU WILL ALWAYS BE SUCCESSFUL AND WONDER WHAT ALL THE FUSS WAS ABOUT.

BASIC RULES

1. All the ingredients should be at room temperature.
2. Use hot water to rinse the bowl and whisk or blender before you start. Dry them thoroughly.
3. Add the oil one drop at a time initially. Don't add it too quickly or the mayonnaise may split and curdle.

MAKING BY HAND

1. Put the egg yolks and lemon juice or wine vinegar in a warm bowl (see above) with the mustard (if using).
2. Beat well with a balloon whisk or hand-held electric whisk until the ingredients are blended and the mixture starts to thicken.
3. Start adding the olive oil gently, one drop at a time initially. Beat continuously until each drop is incorporated and don't rush this stage. When the mayonnaise starts to emulsify, you can add the oil faster and more steadily. Continue beating until you have used all the oil and you have a thick and creamy mayonnaise. Season to taste with salt and pepper.
4. The mayonnaise will keep well in a sealed container in the fridge for 2 days.

USING A BLENDER

1. Blend the egg yolks and lemon juice or vinegar and mustard (if using) on high speed.
2. Add the oil, gently and gradually through the feed tube until the mixture thickens and comes together.
3. Add the remaining oil in a thin steady trickle.

TIP Don't use a strongly flavoured or fruity olive oil – it will taste far too strong.

WHAT TO DO IF IT CURDLES

Don't worry if the mayo splits and curdles. Here's how you can save it.

1. Break another egg yolk into a clean, dry, warm bowl.
2. Start adding the curdled mayonnaise to the yolk, one drop at a time, whisking well until each drop is amalgamated. As you add more and the mayo thickens, you can speed up and add a little extra oil, too, until you reach the desired consistency.

VEGAN MAYONNAISE

MAKES 250ML/9FL OZ
(GENEROUS 1 CUP)
PREP: 10 MINUTES

50ml/2fl oz (scant ¼ cup)
aquafaba (liquid from a
drained tin of chickpeas)
1 tsp mild Dijon mustard
a generous pinch of sea salt
200ml/7fl oz (generous ¾ cup)
organic groundnut (peanut),
light olive or rapeseed oil
1 tbsp white wine vinegar

VARIATIONS

- Use cider vinegar instead
of wine vinegar for a
sweeter flavour.
- Substitute lemon juice for
the vinegar.
- Use avocado oil or
sunflower oil.
- Stir some chopped tarragon
and chives into the finished
mayonnaise.
- For a vegan aioli, stir in
2 crushed garlic cloves at
the end.
- Stir in some vegan pesto and
use it as a dip.

YOU CAN MAKE A DELICIOUS THICK AND SILKY MAYO WITHOUT EGGS BY SUBSTITUTING AQUAFABA (THE DRAINED LIQUID FROM A TIN OF CHICKPEAS). FOR THE BEST RESULTS, ALWAYS CHOOSE AN ORGANIC VEGETABLE OIL (PREFERABLY OLIVE, RAPESEED OR GROUNDNUT) THAT IS LIGHT AND MILD, AS FULL-FLAVOURED ONES CAN TASTE TOO HARSH. YOU CAN MAKE THE MAYONNAISE BY HAND, BUT YOU'LL ALSO END UP WITH A GREAT-TASTING SAUCE IF YOU USE AN ELECTRIC WHISK OR BLENDER.

1. Put the aquafaba, mustard and salt into a blender goblet or a grease-free bowl. Blend them on a high speed or beat them with a hand-held or electric whisk until everything is well combined and frothy.
2. With the blender motor running, start adding the oil slowly in a thin, steady stream through the feed tube. Keep beating until the mixture thickens and has a creamy texture. If using a hand-held whisk, pour the oil very slowly and consistently from a jug and beat continuously.
3. Lastly, beat in the vinegar. Check the seasoning, adding more salt, mustard or vinegar to taste.
4. Transfer the mayonnaise to a bowl and use it immediately, or store in a sealed container in the fridge. It will keep well for up to one week.

**MAKES 120ML/
4FL OZ (½ CUP)
PREP: 5 MINUTES**

120ml/4fl oz (½ cup) mayonnaise
1 tbsp Dijon mustard
freshly ground black pepper

FLAVOURINGS AND ADDITIONS

120ml/4fl oz (½ cup) plain
    Greek yoghurt
1 tbsp lemon juice
a dash of Tabasco, sriracha or
    Worcestershire sauce
chopped fresh herbs, e.g. dill
    or tarragon

VARIATION

• For a sweeter version, try
    using Dijon honey mustard.

DIJONNAISE

ONCE YOU'VE MASTERED A BASIC MAYONNAISE, TRANSFORMING IT INTO DIJONNAISE IS EASY. THIS IS EXTREMELY VERSATILE AND GREAT FOR SERVING WITH CHICKEN, HAM, PORK, BURGERS, SAUSAGES, HOT DOGS, SUBS OR EVEN FRENCH FRIES. AND IT'S BRILLIANT IN SANDWICHES, WRAPS AND MELTING–CHEESE TOASTIES. IT EVEN TASTES DELICIOUS WITH ROASTED VEGETABLES.

1. Mix together the mayonnaise and Dijon mustard in a bowl. Season to taste with black pepper, and add more mayo or mustard until you reach the right consistency and flavour.
2. To take the Dijonnaise to the next level, stir in some yoghurt to make it into a dip or creamy sauce. Add some lemon juice for a fresh zingy taste, or some Tabasco, sriracha or Worcestershire sauce for heat and/or spice. Or stir in some finely chopped fresh herbs for a summery flavour.

TIP This is a delicious way to elevate shop-bought mayo into something more tasty, and it only takes a few minutes plus some store-cupboard ingredients.

AIOLI

**MAKES ABOUT 300G/
10OZ (1¼ CUPS)
PREP: 10 MINUTES**

3 large garlic cloves, peeled
½ tsp sea salt
3 medium free-range egg yolks
juice of ½ lemon
250ml/9fl oz (1 generous cup)
    light olive oil

VARIATIONS

- You can use a full-bodied, fruity-flavoured olive oil for making aioli.
- For a quick cheat's version, just add 2–3 crushed garlic cloves to some ready-made mayo.

THIS INTENSELY GARLIC–FLAVOURED MAYONNAISE IS ONE OF THE GREAT SAUCES OF PROVENCE. IT IS TRADITIONALLY SERVED WITH SALT COD, BOILED EGGS AND RAW OR COOKED VEGETABLES, BUT YOU CAN ADD IT TO SANDWICHES AND WRAPS, SERVE IT AS A DIP FOR VEGETABLE CRUDITÉS OR AN ACCOMPANIMENT FOR CRAB CAKES, A SPANISH OMELETTE OR ARTICHOKES. ANYTHING GOES. AS WITH BASIC HOMEMADE MAYONNAISE, MAKE SURE THAT ALL THE INGREDIENTS ARE AT ROOM TEMPERATURE BEFORE YOU START.

1. Chop the garlic coarsely on a wooden board and then sprinkle it with the salt. Press down on the garlic and salt with the flat blade of the knife to crush it to a thick paste.
2. Transfer the garlic to a clean, dry bowl and add the egg yolks and lemon juice. Beat well with a balloon whisk or hand-held electric whisk until everything is well combined.
3. When it's amalgamated, start slowly adding the olive oil – drop by drop at first, and then in a thin, steady stream – whisking all the time. As the aioli starts to thicken and emulsify, you can speed up the process. You should end up with a thick, glossy sauce.
4. Store in an airtight container in the fridge for up to 2 days.

FLAVOURINGS FOR MAYONNAISE

ONCE YOU HAVE MASTERED THE CLASSIC MAYONNAISE RECIPE, YOU CAN FLAVOUR IT WITH A WIDE RANGE OF INGREDIENTS, DEPENDING ON WHAT YOU LIKE AND HOW YOU INTEND TO SERVE IT. HERE ARE SOME SUGGESTIONS TO INSPIRE YOU.

HARISSA MAYO

For a fiery hot mayo, stir in a dash of harissa paste. Add a little at a time, tasting between each addition, until you get the desired amount of heat.

SRIRACHA MAYO

Add sriracha to taste plus a crushed garlic clove and a dash of lemon or lime juice.

SWEET CHILLI MAYO

Stir in some Thai sweet chilli sauce and loosen the mayo with some Greek yoghurt or soured cream for a creamy texture.

HORSERADISH MAYO

This is great for serving with smoked trout, smoked salmon or rare roast beef. Stir in some prepared horseradish sauce, some snipped fresh chives and a dash of lemon juice.

WASABI MAYO

Stir ½ tablespoon of wasabi paste into a cup of mayonnaise. You could also add a dash of lemon juice or some grated fresh root ginger. Serve with sushi, sashimi, roast beef and smoked fish.

GREEN HERB MAYO

Chop seasonal fresh herbs to colour and flavour a classic mayo. Choose from chives, tarragon, dill, basil, flat-leaf parsley, coriander (cilantro) and sorrel. Add some Greek yoghurt, soured cream or crème fraîche for creaminess, plus a dash of lemon juice and a dusting of paprika or cayenne.

WATERCRESS MAYO

Make homemade mayo (see page 11) and at the end blend in 100g/3½oz of trimmed watercress. Eat this within 24 hours or it will start to lose its lovely fresh green colour. Serve it with poached salmon or chicken breast fillets. You can make rocket (arugula) mayo in the same way.

PESTO MAYO

Stir 1–2 tablespoons of green or red pesto into a cup of mayonnaise. Serve with griddled and roasted vegetables, and potato and pasta salads.

SUN-DRIED TOMATO MAYO

Use sun-dried tomato pesto or finely chopped sun-blush tomatoes to flavour the mayo. Stir in some finely chopped fresh basil and a little soured cream or Greek yoghurt.

BBQ MAYO

Flavour the mayo with your favourite BBQ sauce, adding it a little at a time until you get the required taste. You can spice it up with smoked paprika, onion and garlic powder or a dash of Worcestershire sauce. A few drops of apple cider vinegar will add piquancy. Serve with grilled meat, chicken, shrimp and seafood or pulled jackfruit.

SAFFRON MAYO

Put a pinch of saffron in a small bowl with 1 tablespoon of just-boiled water and set aside for 5 minutes. Stir into a bowl of mayonnaise for a lovely golden colour and subtle flavour.

MARIE ROSE SAUCE

To make this sauce, which is used in prawn (shrimp) cocktails, stir 1–2 tablespoons of tomato ketchup and a dash of Worcestershire sauce into the mayonnaise.

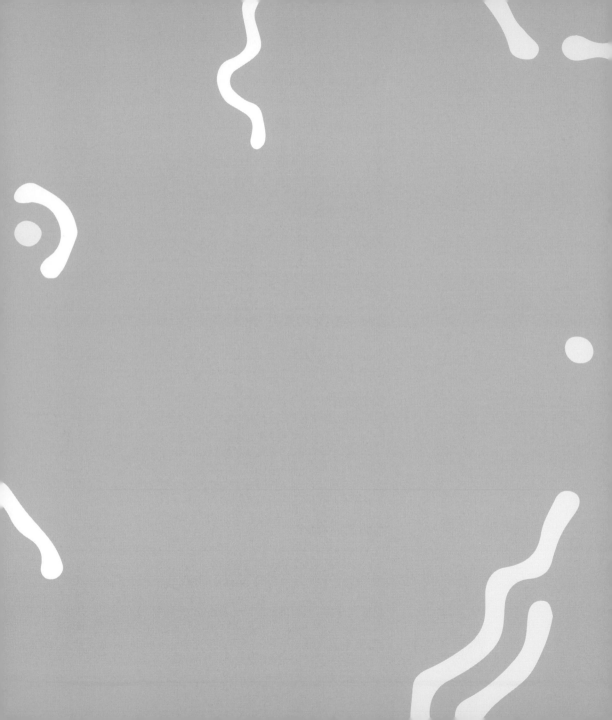

DIPS & DRESSINGS

SERVES 4
PREP: 5 MINUTES
CHILL: 1 HOUR

115g/4oz (½ cup) mayonnaise
2 tbsp sweet pickle relish
2 tbsp tomato ketchup
1 tbsp diced red onion
1 small garlic clove, crushed
1 tsp white wine vinegar or apple
    cider vinegar
a pinch of sweet paprika
sea salt and freshly ground
    black pepper

VARIATIONS

- Spice it up with a dash
  of Tabasco, sriracha or
  chilli paste.
- Substitute sweet piccalilli
  for the sweet pickle.
- To make it less sweet, add
  a dash of lemon juice.

VEGETARIAN

THOUSAND ISLAND DRESSING

THIS SWEET AND TANGY MAYONNAISE—BASED DRESSING IS UNBELIEVABLY VERSATILE AND GOES WAY BEYOND AN ORDINARY SALAD DRESSING. YOU CAN USE IT AS A SPREAD IN SANDWICHES, DRIZZLE IT OVER BURGERS, SERVE IT AS A DIP FOR VEGETABLES AND FRENCH FRIES, OR AS A SAUCE FOR PRAWN COCKTAIL AND SEAFOOD. MIX IT INTO POTATO SALADS OR USE IT TO TOP HARD—BOILED EGGS AND HALVED AVOCADOS. IT'S A GREAT RECIPE TO HAVE IN YOUR REPERTOIRE.

1. Put all the ingredients in a bowl and whisk them together
   until evenly blended.
2. Cover the bowl and chill in the fridge for a minimum of
   1 hour to allow the flavours to develop.
3. You can store this dressing in an airtight container in
   the fridge for at least a week.

SPICY MAYO HUMMUS

**SERVES 4
PREP: 15 MINUTES
COOK: 25-30 MINUTES**

1 × 400g/14oz tin chickpeas (garbanzos), drained, liquid reserved
2–3 garlic cloves, crushed
1 tbsp tahini
juice of 1 small lemon
½ tsp ground cumin
60g/2oz (¼ cup) Chipotle mayonnaise (see page 82)
2 tbsp 0% fat Greek yoghurt
sea salt and freshly ground black pepper
warm pitta triangles or flatbreads, to serve

ROASTED CHICKPEA TOPPING

1 × 400g/14oz tin chickpeas, drained and rinsed
1–2 tbsp olive oil
¼ tsp fine sea salt
½ tsp chilli powder
½ tsp smoked paprika
½ tsp ground cumin

VARIATIONS

- Dust the hummus with smoked paprika or cumin.
- Drizzle some olive oil or lemon juice over the top.
- For a less spicy hummus, use regular mayonnaise.

THIS SPICED, CREAMY HUMMUS TOPPED WITH CRUNCHY ROASTED CHICKPEAS IS THE PERFECT PARTY DIP. YOU CAN KEEP IT IN A SEALED CONTAINER IN THE FRIDGE FOR UP TO THREE DAYS AND ENJOY IT AS A SNACK OR IN PACKED LUNCHES.

1. Preheat the oven to 200°C/180°C fan/400°F/gas mark 6.
2. Make the roasted chickpeas: put the chickpeas in a bowl with the olive oil, salt and ground spices. Toss them lightly until they are evenly coated, then spread them out in a single layer on a baking tray.
3. Roast in the oven for 25–30 minutes, turning once or twice, until they are crisp and golden brown. Watch them carefully towards the end to make sure they don't catch and burn. Remove them from the oven and leave to cool.
4. Make the hummus: rinse the drained chickpeas in a sieve under running cold water and pat them dry with kitchen paper (paper towels). Blitz them to a paste with the garlic, tahini, lemon juice and cumin in a food processor or blender. Add the mayonnaise and yoghurt and blitz until smooth. Season to taste and, if the hummus is too thick, slacken it with a little of the reserved chickpea liquid.
5. Transfer it to a shallow bowl and sprinkle with the roasted chickpeas. Serve with warm pitta triangles or flatbreads.

GUACAMOLE MAYO DIP

SERVES 4
PREP: 10 MINUTES

½ red onion, diced

1 fresh green chilli, diced

1 garlic clove, crushed

½ tsp sea salt flakes

2 ripe avocados

juice of 1 lime

1 medium ripe tomato, deseeded
and diced

a large handful of coriander
(cilantro), chopped

60g/2oz (¼ cup) mayonnaise

freshly ground black pepper

tortilla chips, prawn crackers or
raw vegetable sticks, to serve

VARIATIONS

- Substitute diced spring onions (scallions) for the red onion.
- Use red Thai bird's eye chillies, jalapeños or fiery Scotch bonnets.
- If you don't have a lime, use lemon juice instead.
- If you don't like coriander, try flat-leaf parsley.

ADDING SOME MAYONNAISE TO THIS CLASSIC MEXICAN DIP MAKES IT CREAMY AND FLAVOURFUL, ALBEIT NOT SO AUTHENTIC! YOU CAN ALSO SERVE THIS WITH GRILLED CHICKEN, SALMON OR VEGETABLES, OR EVEN AS A FILLING FOR SANDWICHES AND PITTA POCKETS.

1. Crush the red onion, chilli, garlic and salt to a thick paste in a pestle and mortar.
2. Cut the avocados in half and remove the stones. Scoop out the flesh and place it in a bowl. Mash it coarsely with a fork. Don't worry if there's the odd lump – you don't want the guacamole to be too smooth. Stir in the lime juice.
3. Add the tomato, coriander and the crushed red onion mixture. Mix everything together and then stir in the mayonnaise. Add a grind of black pepper to taste and transfer to a serving bowl.
4. Serve with tortilla chips, prawn crackers or raw vegetable sticks.

TIP You can store the guacamole in a sealed container in the fridge for up to 2 days.

NOTE For a vegan version, use vegan mayo.

450g/1lb raw beetroots (beets),
  trimmed and unpeeled
2 tbsp olive oil, plus extra
  for roasting
2 garlic cloves, peeled
100ml/3½fl oz (scant ½ cup)
  Greek yoghurt
3–4 tbsp mayonnaise
sea salt and freshly ground
  black pepper
warm flatbreads or pitta
  breads, to serve

VARIATIONS

- Use golden beetroots (beets) instead of red.
- Sprinkle with some chopped dill or toasted pine nuts.
- Add a dash of lemon or lime juice.
- Serve with griddled or fried halloumi or even potato chips.

VEGAN OPTION

TURKISH BEETROOT AND MAYO DIP

THIS VIBRANT, COLOURFUL DIP LOOKS AND TASTES SENSATIONAL. SERVE IT WITH PRE-DINNER DRINKS, AT PARTIES OR AS PART OF A MEZZE SPREAD.

1. Preheat the oven to 180°C/160°C fan/350°F/gas mark 4.
2. Take a sheet of foil and place it on a baking tray. Rub the unpeeled beetroots with olive oil and sprinkle them with salt. Place them on the foil and then fold the foil over the top to form a parcel enclosing the beetroots.
3. Bake in the oven for 1 hour, or until the beetroots are cooked and tender. You can test them by piercing them to the centre with the tip of a thin skewer or a sharp knife. Set them aside to cool.
4. When the beetroots are cool enough to handle, peel off and discard the outer skin. Cut the flesh into chunks and place it in a blender or food processor with the olive oil, garlic, Greek yoghurt (reserving a tablespoonful to serve) and mayonnaise. Blitz until it's smooth, then check the seasoning, adding salt and pepper to taste.
5. Transfer the dip to a serving bowl and swirl in the reserved yoghurt. Serve as a dip with warm flatbreads or pitta breads.

TIP If the dip is a little stiff, you can loosen it and make it creamier by adding more yoghurt or mayonnaise.

NOTE For a vegan version, use vegan mayo.

BLUE CHEESE MAYO DRESSING

SERVES 6
PREP: 10 MINUTES

60ml/2fl oz (¼ cup) soured cream
50g/2oz (¼ cup) mayonnaise
50g/2oz blue cheese, crumbled
1 tbsp lemon juice or white
    wine vinegar
3 tbsp buttermilk
a pinch of garlic powder (optional)
sea salt and freshly ground black
    pepper

VARIATIONS

- For a thinner salad dressing, add more buttermilk.
- Sweeten the dressing by adding a pinch of sugar or a little clear honey.
- Add a dash of Worcestershire sauce or a pinch of dry mustard powder.
- Use Greek yoghurt instead of soured cream.

THIS CLASSIC BLUE CHEESE DRESSING IS PERFECT FOR TOSSING CRISP LETTUCE SALADS. YOU CAN MAKE IT THICKER – ADDING MORE CHEESE, SOURED CREAM AND MAYO AND USING LESS BUTTERMILK – AND SERVE IT AS A DIP WITH RAW VEGETABLE STICKS, TORTILLA CHIPS OR A BURGUNDY BEEF FONDUE (SEE PAGE 95). THE BLUE CHEESE YOU USE DEPENDS ON PERSONAL TASTE: ROQUEFORT AND STILTON ARE CRUMBLY AND SALTY, WHEREAS GORGONZOLA OR DANISH BLUE ARE MORE CREAMY.

1. Put the soured cream and mayonnaise into a bowl. Whisk them well until they are blended and then stir in the blue cheese, mashing it slightly with a fork. The mixture doesn't need to be smooth – a slightly crumbly texture is ideal.
2. Add the lemon juice or vinegar and the buttermilk. Mix well, then season with garlic powder (if using), and salt and pepper to taste.
3. Use immediately for dressing salads or store in a sealed container in the fridge for up to 3 days.

ITALIAN CREAMY MAYO DRESSING

SERVES 6
PREP: 5 MINUTES
CHILL: 1 HOUR

115g/4oz (½ cup) mayonnaise
90ml/3fl oz (⅓ cup) olive oil
2 tbsp red wine vinegar
juice of ½ lemon
1 tsp clear honey
¼ red onion, diced
2 garlic cloves, crushed
½ tsp each dried oregano,
    basil, parsley
2 tbsp grated Parmesan cheese
salt and freshly ground black
    pepper

VARIATIONS

- Use caster (superfine) sugar instead of honey.
- Substitute white wine vinegar or apple cider vinegar for the red.
- Use garlic powder instead of fresh garlic.
- Instead of dried herbs, use 1 teaspoon Italian seasoning.
- Stir in some soured cream to make the dressing even more creamy.
- For extra flavour, add some dried red pepper or crushed chilli flakes.

ITALIAN CREAMY DRESSING MADE WITH A MAYONNAISE BASE IS AN AMERICAN CLASSIC – PERFECT FOR SIMPLE SALADS OF LETTUCE, TOMATOES AND CRISPY CROÛTONS.

1. Whisk all the ingredients together in a bowl until they are well combined. Season to taste with salt and pepper. Alternatively, put them in a screw-top jar and shake it vigorously or, for a smooth dressing, blitz them in a blender or food processor until smooth.
2. Chill the dressing in the fridge for at least 1 hour before using it to dress a salad. It will keep well in an airtight container in the fridge for up to 1 week.

NOTE For a vegan version, use vegan mayo and grated cheese, and substitute sugar or agave syrup for the honey.

RANCH DRESSING

SERVES 6-8
PREP: 5 MINUTES
CHILL: 1-2 HOURS

115g/4oz (½ cup) mayonnaise

120ml/4fl oz (½ cup) buttermilk

60ml/2fl oz (¼ cup) soured cream

1 tsp dried dill

½ tsp dried parsley

¼ tsp each garlic powder and
onion powder

a few fresh chives, snipped

juice of ½ lemon

sea salt and freshly ground
black pepper

VARIATIONS

- Add a dash of white wine
  vinegar or apple cider vinegar
  instead of lemon juice.
- Use dried chives instead
  of fresh.
- Use chopped fresh parsley
  and dill.
- Substitute Greek yoghurt for
  the soured cream.
- For a more spicy, strongly
  flavoured dressing, increase
  the onion and garlic powders
  to ½ teaspoon of each.

HOMEMADE RANCH DRESSING TASTES SO MUCH BETTER THAN ANYTHING YOU CAN BUY IN THE SUPERMARKET. YOU CAN USE IT FOR DRESSING SALADS OR REDUCE THE BUTTERMILK TO MAKE IT THICKER THEN SERVE IT AS A DIP WITH RAW VEGETABLE STICKS, BUFFALO WINGS, CRISPY FRIED CHICKEN OR TOFU.

1. Whisk the mayonnaise, buttermilk, soured cream, dried herbs and garlic and onion powders together in a bowl until smooth. Add the chives and whisk in the lemon juice. Season to taste with salt and pepper.
2. Cover the bowl and chill it in the fridge for 1–2 hours before using. This dressing will keep well stored in an airtight container or screw-top jar in the fridge for up to 1 week.

TIP If the dressing seems too thick, thin it with more buttermilk.

SKORDALIA

SERVES 4-6
PREP: 15 MINUTES
SOAK: 5 MINUTES

150g/5oz stale white bread,
   sliced, crusts removed
6 garlic cloves, peeled
½ tsp sea salt crystals
85g/3oz (generous ½ cup)
   blanched almonds
1–2 tsp red wine vinegar
120ml/4fl oz (½ cup) light olive oil
a dash of lemon juice
freshly ground black pepper
pitta or flatbreads, to serve

VARIATION

- Use walnuts instead of
  almonds.

THIS INTENSELY GARLICKY GREEK SAUCE OR DIP IS PREPARED IN A SIMILAR WAY TO A CLASSIC MAYONNAISE BUT WITHOUT THE TRADITIONAL EGG YOLKS. THIS RECIPE USES STALE BREAD, BUT A SMOOTHER SKORDALIA CAN BE MADE WITH POTATOES.

1. Place the bread in a bowl and cover it with cold water. Leave it to soak for 5 minutes, then remove the bread and gently squeeze out any surplus water. Place it in a blender or food processor.
2. While the bread is soaking, grind the garlic and salt to a paste in a pestle and mortar.
3. Add the garlic paste, almonds and vinegar to the bread in the blender or food processor. Pulse until you have a smooth paste. Now, with the motor running, add the olive oil slowly in a thin, steady stream through the feed tube until the skordalia is thick and slightly grainy.
4. Check the seasoning, adding lemon juice, salt and pepper if needed. Serve as a dip with warm pitta or flatbreads, or as an accompaniment to grilled or fried fish, roasted vegetables or hot fritters.

TIP You can also thin the skordalia with a little water to make a sauce.

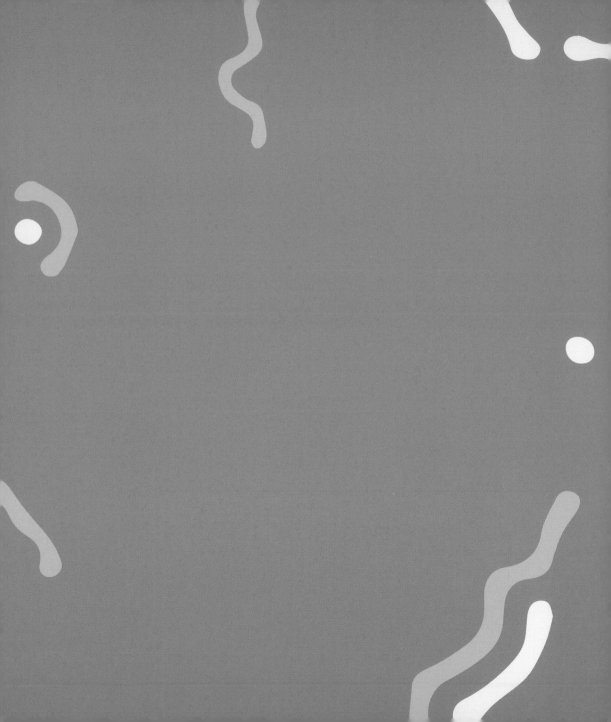

STARTERS, SNACKS & SIDES

2kg/4lb 7oz live mussels in
   their shells
2 tbsp olive oil
3 garlic cloves, crushed
2 shallots, finely chopped
1 celery stick, finely diced
150ml/¼ pint (generous ½ cup)
   dry white wine, e.g.
   Chardonnay or Muscadet
1 fresh red chilli, finely diced
   (optional)
a bunch of parsley, chopped
juice of 1 lemon
60ml/2fl oz (¼ cup) double
   (heavy) cream
salt and freshly ground
   black pepper
French fries, to serve
Homemade mayonnaise (see page
   11) or Aioli (see page 17), to serve

VARIATIONS

- Substitute crème fraîche for
  double cream if you like a
  slightly sharper sauce.
- Alternatively, add extra
  cream for a really creamy,
  unctuous sauce.
- Serve with Dijonnaise (see
  page 16).

MOULES FRITES WITH MAYO

THIS CLASSIC DISH OF MUSSELS IN A GARLICKY, CREAMY, WHITE WINE SAUCE IS DELICIOUS SERVED IN THE FRENCH OR BELGIAN STYLE WITH A LARGE PLATTER OF HOT CRISPY FRENCH FRIES AND A BOWL OF HOMEMADE MAYO OR AIOLI.

1. Prepare the mussels: place them in a large bowl of cold water and discard any that are cracked or stay open. They should all be tightly shut. Pull off any wispy beards and scrub the shells.
2. Set a large, lidded saucepan over a low to medium heat, add the oil and sweat the garlic, shallots and celery, stirring occasionally, for 5 minutes, or until they are tender.
3. Add the wine and mussels to the pan then cover it with a lid. Simmer the mussels gently for 3–4 minutes, shaking the pan once or twice, until they open. Remove and discard any that remain closed.
4. Add the chilli (if using), parsley, lemon juice and cream, and bring to the boil. Season to taste with salt and pepper.
5. Divide the mussels between four shallow serving bowls and eat them immediately with plenty of French fries and a bowl of mayonnaise or aioli for dipping. Provide a spare plate for the empty mussel shells.

NOTE It is very important to prepare the mussels as outlined in the method above. Do not skimp on this.

**SERVES 3-4
PREP: 15 MINUTES
CHILL: 30 MINUTES
COOK: 6 MINUTES**

450g/1lb fresh crab meat
2 red bird's eye chillies, diced
4 spring onions (scallions), chopped
1 stalk lemongrass, peeled and
thinly sliced
2 garlic cloves, crushed
a large handful of coriander
(cilantro), plus extra for garnish
50g/2oz (1 cup) fresh white
breadcrumbs
2 tsp nam pla (Thai fish sauce)
2 tbsp mayonnaise
plain (all-purpose) flour, for dusting
oil for shallow-frying

DIPPING SAUCE

2 tbsp rice vinegar
1 tsp sugar
1 tsp dark soy sauce
1 red bird's eye chilli, shredded
juice of 1 lime

VARIATIONS

- Add some thinly sliced kaffir
lime leaves to the crab cake
mixture.
- Serve simply with Thai sweet
chilli sauce.
- If you don't like a lot of heat, use
just one chilli in the crab cake
mixture or discard the seeds.

THAI CRAB CAKES

THESE CRISP LITTLE CRAB CAKES ARE HOT AND SPICY AND MAKE A DELICIOUS FIRST COURSE. THE MAYONNAISE MAY SEEM SURPRISING BUT IT BINDS THE MIXTURE TOGETHER AND ADDS A HINT OF CREAMINESS. THIS RECIPE SUGGESTS SERVING THE CRAB CAKES WITH A DIPPING SAUCE, BUT A HOT SRIRACHA MAYO (SEE PAGE 18) OR THE CURRIED CORIANDER MAYO (SEE PAGE 49) WOULD ALSO WORK.

1. Pulse the crab meat, chillies, spring onions, lemongrass, garlic, coriander leaves, breadcrumbs, nam pla and mayonnaise in a blender or food processor until just combined. Do not blitz for too long – the mixture should still have some texture.
2. Divide the mixture into 12 equal-sized portions and shape them with your hands into little patties. Dust them very lightly with flour, then cover and chill them in the fridge for at least 30 minutes.
3. Meanwhile, make the dipping sauce: heat the rice vinegar and sugar in a small pan set over a low to medium heat, stirring until the sugar dissolves and the mixture is syrupy. Stir in the soy sauce, chilli and lime juice and remove the pan from the heat. Set it aside to cool.
4. Heat just enough oil to cover the base of a large frying pan (skillet) set over a medium to high heat. Fry the crab cakes for 3 minutes on each side, turning carefully with a spatula so they keep their shape, until they are golden brown.
5. Serve the crab cakes hot from the pan with the dipping sauce, with salad leaves or fresh coriander sprigs.

NOTE If you can't buy fresh crab meat, you can use frozen and thawed crab meat or even tinned or bottled crab meat.

2 tsp olive oil
a bunch of spring onions
    (scallions), thinly sliced
2 garlic cloves, crushed
400g/14oz spinach, washed
    and trimmed
100g/3½oz feta cheese, crumbled
a handful of dill, finely chopped
115g/4oz filo (phyllo) pastry
60g/2oz (¼ cup) unsalted butter
3 tbsp sesame seeds
salt and freshly ground
    black pepper

FETA AND DILL MAYO

115g/4oz (½ cup) mayonnaise
120ml/4fl oz (½ cup) Greek
    yoghurt or kefir
50g/2oz feta cheese, crumbled
½ tsp dried dill
freshly ground black pepper

VARIATIONS

- Brush the filo pastry with olive oil instead of butter.
- Use freshly chopped dill in the mayo dip.

VEGETARIAN

SPANAKOPITA CRISPY FILO ROLLS

CRISP ROLLS OF FILO PASTRY FILLED WITH SPINACH AND FETA ARE DELICIOUS TO SERVE AS SNACKS OR CANAPÉS. THEY ARE A LITTLE TIME CONSUMING TO MAKE BUT WELL WORTH THE EFFORT FOR SPECIAL OCCASIONS.

1. Preheat the oven to 180°C/160°C fan/350°F/gas mark 4. Line 2 baking trays with non-stick baking parchment.
2. Heat the oil in a pan set over a low heat and gently cook the spring onions and garlic for 5 minutes, or until tender.
3. Place the spinach in a colander and stand it in the sink. Pour boiling water over the leaves until they wilt. Allow the water to drain away, then press down firmly on the leaves with a saucer to squeeze out excess water. Chop the spinach and transfer to a bowl with the spring onions, feta and dill. Mix gently and season with salt and pepper.
4. Place the sheets of filo pastry on a clean work surface and cut each one in half lengthwise so you have 2 rectangles. Cut each rectangle into 4 pieces, so you end up with 8 rectangles from each sheet.
5. Melt the butter in a pan and brush it lightly over one of the pastry rectangles. Smear a little of the spinach filling along one long side, leaving a thin edge, and then roll up the pastry tightly like a cigar. Place the roll seam-side down on one of the baking trays. Repeat with the other filo rectangles and filling.
6. Brush the filo rolls with the remaining melted butter and sprinkle them with sesame seeds. Bake in the oven for 12–15 minutes, until they are crisp and golden brown.
7. Meanwhile, make the feta and dill mayo: mix all the ingredients together until they are smooth, adding black pepper to taste. Chill the mayo in the fridge until you're ready to serve it with the crisp filo rolls.

CELERIAC REMOULADE

SERVES 4-6
PREP: 15 MINUTES
STAND: 15-30 MINUTES

450g/1lb celeriac (celery root)
juice of 1 lemon
8 tbsp mayonnaise
2 tbsp Dijon mustard
2 tbsp crème fraîche
a few sprigs of flat-leaf
   parsley, finely chopped
salt and freshly ground
   black pepper
chopped fresh parsley and poppy
   seeds, for sprinkling
   (optional)

VARIATIONS

- Use double (heavy) cream
  instead of crème fraîche.
- Sprinkle with chopped
  nuts, e.g. hazelnuts, pecans
  or walnuts.

IN THE WINTER WHEN WE CRAVE A SALAD BUT DON'T FEEL LIKE MUNCHING ON LEAVES, THIS CLASSIC FRENCH SALAD OF CRISP CELERIAC IN A CREAMY MAYONNAISE IS THE PERFECT COMFORT FOOD. THIS IS TRADITIONALLY SERVED WITH BOILED OR CURED HAM. FOR THE BEST RESULTS, USE HOMEMADE MAYONNAISE.

1. Quickly peel the celeriac and then cut the peeled root into matchstick-thin sticks, adding them to a bowl with the lemon juice to keep them creamy white in colour.
2. Mix the mayonnaise, mustard and crème fraîche in a large bowl until they are well combined. Season with salt and pepper to taste and stir in the parsley.
3. Gently but thoroughly fold the celeriac sticks into the mayo mixture, until all the sticks are coated. Cover the bowl and set the remoulade aside for 15–30 minutes to allow the flavours to mingle.
4. Serve sprinkled with chopped parsley and poppy seeds (if using).

TIP It's important to work fast when preparing celeriac to prevent it discolouring. Have the lemon juice ready in a bowl before you start preparing the celeriac.

NOTE Some French chefs recommend blanching the celeriac: put the lemony celeriac sticks into a pan of boiling acidulated water (water with lemon juice added). As soon as it returns to the boil, drain the sticks in a colander and then rinse them under cold running water. Pat them dry with kitchen paper (paper towels) before mixing them with the mustardy mayo.

CRISPY PARMESAN AND TRUFFLE OVEN CHIPS

SERVES 3-4
PREP: 15 MINUTES
COOK: 20-25 MINUTES

4 medium potatoes, peeled
2 tbsp olive oil
100g/3½oz (1 cup) grated
    Parmesan
truffle oil, for drizzling
sea salt and freshly ground
    black pepper

TRUFFLE MAYO

225g/8oz (1 cup) mayonnaise
1–2 tsp truffle oil
1 garlic clove, crushed
a squeeze of lemon juice (optional)

VARIATIONS

- Instead of cutting the potatoes into chips, slice them thinly.
- If you love truffles, drizzle more truffle oil over the chips before serving.
- If you don't like garlic, omit it from the mayo.

THESE CRISP, GOLDEN OVEN CHIPS HAVE THE WONDERFUL AROMA AND FLAVOUR OF TRUFFLES. FOR THE BEST RESULTS, USE A HIGH-QUALITY TRUFFLE OIL. SERVE THE CHIPS AS A SPECIAL SNACK OR AS A SIDE DISH WITH STEAKS.

1. Make the truffle mayo: in a bowl, mix together the mayonnaise, 1 teaspoon of truffle oil and the garlic. Taste it and if you think it needs more truffle oil, add another teaspoon. Add lemon juice (if using) and season with salt and pepper. Cover and chill in the fridge until required.
2. Preheat the oven to 230°C/210°C fan/450°F/gas mark 8.
3. Cut the potatoes into fingers approximately 5mm/¼in thick. Tip them into a large, lidded pan of boiling water and parboil them for 3 minutes. Drain them in a colander and set them aside for a few minutes to dry, then pat them dry with kitchen paper (paper towels).
4. Return the potatoes to the warm saucepan and add the olive oil. Season them with salt and pepper and cover the pan with a lid. Shake the pan until the potatoes are coated all over with the seasoned oil. Add more oil if needed.
5. Spread out the potatoes in a single layer on a large baking tray and bake them in the preheated oven for 15–20 minutes, until they are golden brown and crisp. Remove the baking tray from the oven and turn the potatoes over twice during cooking so they brown evenly.
6. Drizzle or spray the potatoes with truffle oil and sprinkle them with a little Parmesan, then return them to the oven for 2 minutes, or until the cheese melts.
7. Pile the chips on to a serving plate or into a large shallow bowl and sprinkle them with the remaining Parmesan. Serve them piping hot with the truffle mayo.

GREEN FALAFELS WITH HARISSA MAYO

MAKES ABOUT 20
SOAK: OVERNIGHT
PREP: 20 MINUTES
CHILL: 1 HOUR
COOK: 12-15 MINUTES

300g/10oz (generous 1¼ cups)
   dried chickpeas (garbanzos)
6 spring onions (scallions), sliced
a bunch of coriander (cilantro),
   chopped
a bunch of flat-leaf parsley,
   chopped
a handful of mint, chopped
4 garlic cloves, crushed
1½ tbsp chickpea (gram) flour
1 tsp baking powder
1 tsp salt
1 tsp ground cumin
1 tsp ground coriander
a pinch of cayenne pepper
freshly ground black pepper
white sesame seeds, for sprinkling
sunflower or vegetable oil, for
   deep-frying

HARISSA MAYO
225g/8oz (1 cup) mayonnaise
1–2 tsp harissa paste
½ tsp paprika

VARIATIONS
- Add some chilli to the falafel.
- Add a little grated lemon zest.
- Serve with Sweet chilli mayo
  (see page 18).

THESE FALAFELS ARE EASY TO MAKE AND CAN BE SERVED AS SNACKS OR AS A FILLING FOR PITTA OR WRAPS. THE HARISSA MAYO GIVES THEM A SPICY KICK. THEY KEEP WELL IN AN AIRTIGHT CONTAINER IN THE FRIDGE FOR UP TO 3 DAYS, OR CAN BE FROZEN.

1. Put the chickpeas in a bowl and cover them with plenty of cold water. Leave them to soak overnight. The following day, drain them and pat them dry with kitchen paper (paper towels).
2. Blitz the chickpeas in a food processor with the spring onions, herbs and garlic. Add the chickpea flour, baking powder, salt and spices, and pulse until everything is well combined. If it's too dry, moisten it with a little cold water. Add some black pepper and blitz again. Do not over-process – the texture should be coarse rather than smooth.
3. Dampen your hands then take a spoonful of the mixture and shape it into a small ball. Repeat until all the mixture is used up. Roll the balls in sesame seeds, then cover them and chill them in the fridge for at least 1 hour.
4. Meanwhile, make the harissa mayo: mix the mayonnaise with 1 teaspoon of harissa and then taste. If you like it really fiery, add more harissa. Stir in the paprika, then cover and chill the mayo in the fridge until required.
5. Pour the oil into a deep heavy-based saucepan to a depth of at least 7.5cm/3in. Set the pan over a medium to high heat and when the temperature reaches 180°C/350°F (use a sugar thermometer to check), add the falafels a few at a time, without overcrowding the pan. Deep-fry them for 4–5 minutes until they are crisp and golden. Remove them with a slotted spoon and drain them on kitchen paper.
6. Serve the falafels hot or cold with the harissa mayo.

**SERVES 4-6
PREP: 15 MINUTES
MARINATE: 2 HOURS
COOK: 25-30 MINUTES**

spray oil
8 chicken wings, each cut in
   2 (16 wing pieces)
1 tsp smoked paprika
½ tsp ground cumin
½ tsp ground coriander
a pinch of dried thyme
1 tbsp grated fresh root ginger
2 garlic cloves, crushed
4 tbsp hot sauce
2 tbsp clear honey
freshly ground black pepper

BLUE CHEESE MAYO

115g/4oz (½ cup) mayonnaise
60ml/2fl oz (¼ cup) Greek yoghurt
50g/2oz blue cheese (Roquefort,
   Stilton or Danish Blue), crumbled
a squeeze of lemon juice

VARIATIONS

- Make the marinade more
  spicy: try chilli powder,
  cayenne or paprika.
- Add some seedy mustard,
  or lemon zest and juice.
- Use boned chicken thighs
  instead of wings.
- Serve with BBQ mayo (see
  page 19) or Sriracha mayo
  (see page 18).

BUFFALO WINGS WITH BLUE CHEESE MAYO

YOU CAN USE ANY HOT SAUCE TO MAKE THESE SPICY CHICKEN WINGS. THEY ARE GREAT FOR SERVING WITH PRE–DINNER DRINKS OR AS SNACKS AND PARTY NIBBLES. THIS RECIPE SUGGESTS SERVING THEM WITH A BLUE CHEESE MAYO, BUT YOU COULD ALSO USE A THICK RANCH DRESSING (SEE PAGE 30) AS A DIP.

1. Line a large baking tray with kitchen foil and spray it lightly with oil.
2. Put the chicken wings in a bowl and spray them lightly with oil. In another bowl, mix together the ground spices, thyme, ginger, garlic, hot sauce and honey. Grind in some black pepper and pour the mixture over the wings. Turn them gently until they are completely coated.
3. Cover the bowl and leave the wings to marinate in the fridge for at least 2 hours – or overnight.
4. When you're ready to cook the wings, preheat the oven to 200°C/180°C fan/400°F/gas mark 6.
5. Arrange the wings in a single layer on the baking tray, spooning any leftover marinade over the top. Bake them in the oven for 25–30 minutes, turning them once or twice so they are coated with the marinade, until they are sticky and a deep golden brown.
6. Meanwhile, make the blue cheese mayo: mix together the mayonnaise and yoghurt in a bowl. Crumble in the blue cheese and stir until it is well combined, mashing it into the mayonnaise mixture. Add a dash of lemon juice to taste and chill the mayo in the fridge for 15 minutes.
7. Serve the buffalo wings hot from the oven with the blue cheese mayo on the side.

MAKES 8
PREP: 20 MINUTES
COOK: 5 MINUTES

2 tsp sunflower oil

2 red (bell) peppers, deseeded
and shredded

1 large carrot, cut into thin
matchsticks

2cm/1in piece fresh root
ginger, diced

100g/3½oz spring greens or
spinach, shredded

100g/3½oz (scant 1 cup)
beansprouts

300g/10oz cooked peeled
prawns (shrimp)

2 tbsp light soy sauce

1 small ripe avocado, peeled,
stoned (pitted) and diced

a handful of coriander
(cilantro), chopped

8 round rice paper wrappers

SWEET CHILLI MAYO

115g/4oz (½ cup) mayonnaise

3 tbsp Thai sweet chilli sauce

VARIATIONS

- Use nam pla (Thai fish sauce)
  instead of soy sauce.
- Add some sliced radishes or
  mooli (daikon).
- Use cooked chicken instead
  of prawns.

SHRIMP AND AVOCADO SPRING ROLLS

THESE FRESH-TASTING SPRING ROLLS ARE EASY TO MAKE AND DELICIOUS AS A SNACK SERVED WITH SWEET CHILLI MAYO. YOU CAN BUY RICE PAPER WRAPPERS IN ORIENTAL STORES, DELIS AND MANY SUPERMARKETS.

1. Make the sweet chilli mayo: put the mayonnaise and sweet chilli sauce in a bowl and whisk them together until well combined.
2. Heat the oil in a wok or large frying pan (skillet) set over a high heat. Stir-fry the peppers, carrot and ginger for 2 minutes, then add the greens, beansprouts and prawns and stir-fry for 2 more minutes. Remove from the heat and stir in the soy sauce, avocado and coriander.
3. Fill a bowl with cold water and position it near you while you assemble the spring rolls. Dip a rice paper wrapper into the water until it's pliable. Lay it flat on a clean work surface and spoon some of the prawn and vegetable filling on to it, leaving a broad border around the edge.
4. Fold the sides of the wrapper over the filling to enclose it and then roll it up like a burrito. Repeat with the remaining wrappers and filling. Serve the spring rolls with the sweet chilli mayo for dipping.

2 tbsp olive oil

50g/2oz spinach leaves, washed, trimmed and shredded

100g/3½oz (¾ cup) tinned black beans, rinsed and drained

100g/3½oz (1 cup) grated vegan cheese

2 spring onions (scallions), thinly sliced

1 red chilli, diced

2 large flour tortillas

sea salt flakes and freshly ground black pepper

VEGAN SMASHED AVOCADO MAYO

1 ripe avocado, peeled and stoned (pitted)

1 garlic clove, crushed

a pinch of dried crushed chilli flakes

juice of ½ lime

115g/4oz (½ cup) Vegan mayonnaise (see page 13)

VARIATIONS

- Use tinned refried beans or kidney beans instead of black beans.
- Serve with Guacamole mayo dip (see page 24) or salsa or vegan non-dairy yoghurt.

VEGAN

VEGAN BLACK BEAN QUESADILLAS

CRISPY GOLDEN QUESADILLAS FILLED WITH A VEGAN BLACK BEAN AND SPINACH MIXTURE ARE SURPRISINGLY QUICK AND EASY TO MAKE.

1. Make the smashed avocado mayo: coarsely mash the avocado, garlic and chilli flakes in a bowl until they are well combined but still slightly lumpy. Stir in the lime juice and mayonnaise.
2. Heat 1 tablespoon of oil in a large non-stick frying pan (skillet) set over a medium heat and when it's hot, add the spinach and cook it, stirring, for 1–2 minutes until it wilts.
3. Transfer the spinach to a bowl and mix it with the beans, grated cheese, spring onions and chilli. Stir well and season to taste with salt and pepper.
4. Spread half the mixture over half a tortilla but not right up to the edge. Fold the other half of the tortilla over the top of the filling and press the edges firmly together to seal them. Repeat with the other tortilla and the remaining filling.
5. Heat the remaining oil in the frying pan set over a medium heat. Add the tortillas and cook for 3 minutes, or until they are golden and crisp underneath.
6. Flip them over and cook the other side for 2–3 minutes, until they are golden brown and the cheese is melting.
7. Slide them out of the pan on to a board and cut them into wedges. Sprinkle them with sea salt and serve with the smashed avocado mayo.

NOTE Non-vegans can use grated Cheddar or Monterey Jack cheese in the filling.

TOFU KEBABS WITH SATAY MAYO

SERVES 4
PREP: 10 MINUTES
MARINATE: 30 MINUTES
COOK: 5 MINUTES

200g/7oz firm tofu, cubed
1 green (bell) pepper, deseeded
  and cut into chunks
1 red or yellow (bell) pepper,
  deseeded and cut into chunks
1 red onion, cut into wedges
spray olive oil
a few sprigs of coriander
  (cilantro), chopped

MARINADE

2 tbsp light soy sauce
2 garlic cloves, crushed
1 tbsp tomato paste
1 tsp clear honey

SATAY MAYO

115g/4oz (½ cup) Vegan mayonnaise
  (see page 13)
2 tbsp satay sauce
a squeeze of lime juice
2 tbsp Greek yoghurt (optional)

VARIATIONS

- Serve with Wasabi mayo
  (see page 18).
- Try courgette (zucchini) or
  aubergine (eggplant) chunks,
  button mushrooms.
- Instead of marinated tofu, use
  cubed halloumi cheese and
  drizzle with sriracha.

TOFU HAS A BLAND, DELICATE FLAVOUR AND THIS RECIPE EXPLAINS HOW TO MARINATE IT BEFORE COOKING. SERVE IT WITH A SPICY SATAY MAYO DIP.

1. Mix together the marinade ingredients in a small bowl. Add the tofu cubes and stir them into the marinade until they are lightly coated all over. Set the bowl aside for 30 minutes.
2. Thread the tofu, peppers and red onion alternately on to 4 long or 8 short skewers and spray them lightly with oil.
3. Cook the kebabs on a hot griddle pan or barbecue or under a preheated grill (broiler) for about 5 minutes, turning them occasionally, until the vegetables are tender and slightly charred at the edges and the tofu is golden.
4. Meanwhile, make the satay mayo: put the mayonnaise in a bowl and stir in the satay sauce until they are well blended. Add the lime juice and if the mayo is too thick, loosen it with the yoghurt.
5. Serve the kebabs sprinkled with coriander, with the satay mayo for dipping.

TIP If using bamboo skewers, soak them in water for 30 minutes to prevent them burning on the grill or in the griddle pan.

ONION BHAJIS WITH CURRIED CORIANDER MAYO

SERVES 4-6
PREP: 10 MINUTES
COOK: 10-15 MINUTES

150g/5oz (scant 2 cups) chickpea
(gram) flour
½ tsp baking powder
1 tsp ground turmeric
1 tsp ground cumin
1 tsp ground coriander
1 tsp paprika
½ tsp chilli powder (optional)
a bunch of coriander
(cilantro), chopped
150ml/¼ pint (generous ½ cup)
cold water
4 onions, thinly sliced
vegetable oil, for deep-frying
sea salt, for sprinkling

CURRIED CORIANDER MAYO

225g/8oz (1 cup) mayonnaise
1–2 tbsp curry paste
juice of ½ lime
a handful of coriander (cilantro),
finely chopped

VARIATIONS

- Serve with Indian pickles,
  cucumber yoghurt raita
  flavoured with mint, and
  mango chutney.
- Add a teaspoon of fennel seeds
  and a diced fresh chilli to the
  bhaji batter.

HOMEMADE CRISP AND GOLDEN SPICED ONION BHAJIS ARE A WONDERFUL TREAT. SERVE THEM AS PART OF AN INDIAN–THEMED DINNER OR AS A SNACK OR PARTY FOOD. THEY ARE EASY TO MAKE AND EVERYONE LOVES THEM.

1. Make the curried coriander mayo: put the mayonnaise in a bowl and stir in 1 tablespoon of curry paste. If it's not hot enough for you add some more. Stir in the lime juice and coriander, then cover and chill the mayo in the fridge until needed.
2. Put the flour, baking powder, ground spices and coriander in a bowl. Stir well, then whisk in the cold water to make a batter. If it seems too stiff, add a little more water. Gently stir the sliced onions into the batter to coat them all over.
3. Pour the oil into a deep, heavy-based saucepan to a depth of about 7.5cm/3in. Set the pan over a medium to high heat. When the oil temperature reaches 180°C/350°F (use a sugar thermometer to check) start adding heaped tablespoons of the onion batter. Add them carefully, a few at a time so as not to overcrowd the pan, rather than dropping them in, so the oil does not spit and splatter.
4. Fry the bhajis for 3–4 minutes, turning them occasionally, until they are golden brown and crisp all over. Remove them with a slotted spoon, drain them on kitchen paper (paper towels) and keep them warm. Cook the remaining bhajis in the same way.
5. Serve the bhajis piping hot and sprinkled with sea salt, with the curried coriander mayo.

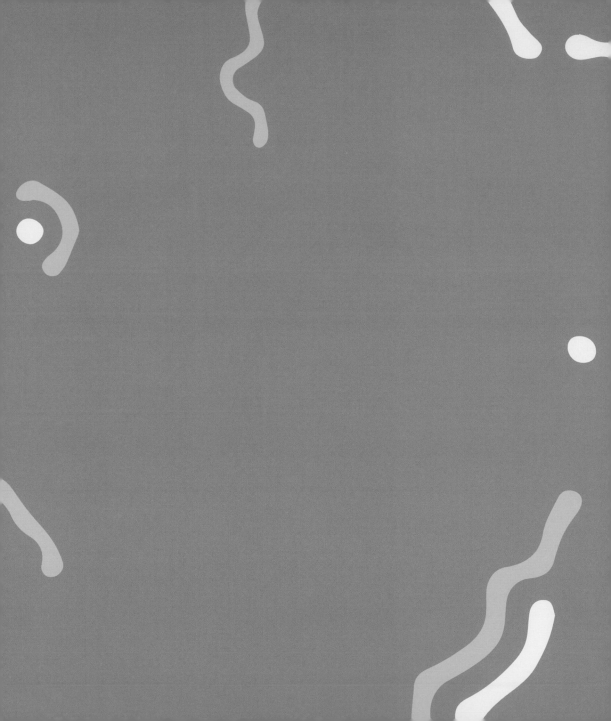

SANDWICHES & LIGHT MEALS

1 red (bell) pepper, deseeded and
   thinly sliced
1 large carrot, cut into thin
   matchsticks
4 radishes, thinly sliced
1 small ridged (Persian) cucumber,
   thinly sliced
4 tbsp rice vinegar
4 tbsp caster (superfine) sugar
1 tbsp nam pla (Thai fish sauce)
4 small baguettes (French sticks)
1 small red onion, thinly sliced
sea salt and freshly ground
   black pepper

BEEF FILLING

1 tbsp olive oil
300g/10oz (scant 1½ cups) minced
   (ground) beef (5% fat)
3 garlic cloves, crushed
1 red bird's eye chilli, diced
a handful of coriander
   (cilantro), chopped

SRIRACHA MAYO

115g/4oz (½ cup) mayonnaise
2 spring onions (scallions), diced
1–2 tbsp sriracha (according
   to taste)

BANH MI WITH SRIRACHA MAYO

THIS VIETNAMESE BAGUETTE TAKES A WHILE TO MAKE BUT IT'S WELL WORTH THE EFFORT. YOU CAN PREPARE BOTH THE MAYO AND THE BEEF FILLING IN ADVANCE.

1. Make the sriracha mayo: mix all the ingredients together in a bowl and season to taste with a little salt. Cover the bowl and chill the mayo in the fridge until you're ready to assemble the baguettes.
2. Mix together the red pepper, carrot, radishes and cucumber in a glass bowl. Heat the rice vinegar and sugar in a small pan set over a low to medium heat, stirring until the sugar dissolves. Bring to the boil and take the pan off the heat. Stir in the nam pla and pour the mixture over the prepared vegetables. Leave it to stand for at least 1 hour.
3. Just before you're ready to serve, make the beef filling: heat the oil in a frying pan (skillet) over a medium to high heat. Add the beef and cook, stirring, for 3–4 minutes until the meat is browned all over. Stir in the garlic and chilli and cook for 2–3 minutes more. Stir in the coriander and check the seasoning, adding salt and pepper if needed.
4. Cut the baguettes in half lengthwise and scoop out and discard most of the soft bread in the centre to leave a crusty outer shell. Spread sriracha mayo over half of each baguette and spoon the beef filling over it. Top with the red pepper and carrot mixture and the red onion slices. Cover with the baguette tops, pressing them down firmly to enclose the filling. Serve immediately.

TIP For the best results, use the finest-quality lean minced beef you can find. Best of all is to mince some lean sirloin or rump steak.

SERVES 4
PREP: 15 MINUTES

4 slices sourdough or
ciabatta bread
1 ripe avocado, peeled, stoned
(pitted) and thinly sliced
350g/12oz sushi-grade tuna, diced
zest of 1 lime, thinly shredded
pickled ginger, to garnish
a few drops of toasted sesame oil
black or white sesame seeds,
for sprinkling
a few fresh chives, snipped
sea salt flakes and freshly ground
black pepper
pickled red onions, to serve
(optional)

MISO MAYO

115g/4oz (½ cup) mayonnaise
1 tbsp white miso paste
a squeeze of lime juice

VARIATIONS

- Add soy sauce and grated
  ginger or a crushed garlic
  clove to the miso mayo.
- Sweeten the miso mayo with
  clear honey to taste.
- Use sushi-grade salmon
  instead of tuna.
- Smash the avocado with a fork
  and spread it over the toasts.
- Top with thinly sliced radish
  or some capers.

MISO MAYO TUNA TOASTS

THE TUNA IN THIS RECIPE IS SERVED UNCOOKED, SO IT'S IMPORTANT TO USE THE FRESHEST AND BEST-QUALITY SUSHI-GRADE TUNA YOU CAN FIND FOR MAKING THESE DELICIOUS UMAMI-FLAVOURED TOASTS. SERVE THEM WITH SALAD FOR A LIGHT MEAL OR HEALTHY BRUNCH, OR CUT THEM INTO SMALLER PIECES AND ENJOY THEM AS AN APPETIZER OR AS PARTY SNACKS.

1. Make the mayo: mix together the mayonnaise and miso paste in a bowl. (If it is too thick, you can thin it with a little Greek yoghurt.) Add lime juice to taste.
2. Lightly toast the bread on both sides on a griddle pan and then cut each slice in half. Top with the sliced avocado.
3. Gently stir the diced tuna into the miso mayo (you may not need it all) and pile it on top of the avocado toasts. Sprinkle with the lime zest and pickled ginger.
4. Season the toasts lightly with sea salt flakes and black pepper, then drizzle them with sesame oil. For the finishing touches, sprinkle with sesame seeds and chives. Serve immediately while the toast is warm with pickled red onions (if using).

TIP Any sushi-grade tuna is OK to use, but if you can buy ahi tuna from your fishmonger, do try it.

500g/1lb 2oz cooked chicken, skinned, boned and cut into pieces

CURRIED MAYO

6 tbsp mayonnaise

3–4 tbsp Greek yoghurt or crème fraîche

2 tsp curry powder or mild curry paste

a pinch of ground turmeric

a pinch of cayenne pepper

2 tbsp mango chutney

3 tbsp sultanas (golden raisins)

a handful of coriander (cilantro), chopped

a good squeeze of lemon juice

salt and freshly ground black pepper

VARIATIONS

- Use diced, dried ready-to-eat apricots, raisins or cranberries instead of sultanas.
- Use chopped fresh parsley instead of coriander.
- Add some thinly sliced spring onions (scallions).
- Substitute cooked turkey for the chicken.
- Sprinkle with toasted flaked almonds.

CORONATION CHICKEN

SERVE THIS CURRIED CHICKEN AND MAYO MIXTURE AS A FILLING FOR SANDWICHES, A TOPPING FOR BAKED POTATOES, OR TO ACCOMPANY A SALAD. IT'S QUICK AND EASY TO MAKE AND A GREAT WAY TO USE UP LEFTOVER ROAST OR POACHED CHICKEN.

1. Make the mayo: put all the ingredients in a medium-sized bowl and mix them together well. Check the seasoning, and add more curry powder, ground spices or lemon juice to taste.
2. Fold the chicken into the mayo. If the mayo is too stiff, loosen it with more yoghurt or crème fraîche.
3. Serve with a salad and new potatoes or use as a topping for toasties or jacket potatoes, or a filling for sandwiches, wraps and pitta pockets.

VEGAN JACKFRUIT WRAPS WITH MANGO MAYO

SERVES 4
PREP: 20 MINUTES
COOK: 25-30 MINUTES

2 tbsp sunflower oil

1 red onion, finely chopped

2 garlic cloves, crushed

1 large sweet potato, peeled and diced

600g/1lb 5oz tinned green jackfruit, drained and shredded with a fork

1–2 tsp curry paste

400g/14oz (2 cups) tinned black beans, rinsed and drained

240ml/8fl oz (1 cup) tinned coconut milk

100g/3½oz baby spinach leaves

4 large naan breads

a few crisp lettuce leaves, shredded

½ small red onion, thinly sliced

a few sprigs of coriander (cilantro), chopped

4 tbsp dairy-free yoghurt, e.g. coconut

sea salt and freshly ground black pepper

MANGO MAYO

115g/4oz (½ cup) Vegan mayonnaise (see page 13)

2 ripe mangoes, peeled, stoned (pitted) and diced

2–3 tsp hot sauce, e.g. sriracha

1 tsp rice vinegar

½ tsp caster (superfine) sugar

juice of ½ lime

SHREDDED TINNED JACKFRUIT IS OFTEN USED INSTEAD OF MEAT IN VEGAN BURGERS, WRAPS AND STIR-FRIES. IT HAS A GREAT TEXTURE AND ABSORBS SPICY FLAVOURINGS. THIS RECIPE USES A COMBO OF CURRY PASTE, GARLIC AND COCONUT MILK.

1. Make the mango mayo: pulse all the ingredients in a blender or food processor until you have a smooth mixture. Scrape it into a bowl, taste it and add more hot sauce, sugar or lime juice if needed. Cover the bowl and set it aside.

2. Heat the oil in a large frying pan (skillet) set over a low to medium heat and cook the onion and garlic, stirring occasionally, for 6–8 minutes until they are tender but not browned. Stir in the sweet potato and jackfruit and cook for 5 minutes. Stir in the curry paste. Preheat the oven to 200°C/180°C fan/400°F/gas mark 6.

3. Add the beans and coconut milk and simmer the mixture gently for 10–15 minutes until the vegetables are cooked and the liquid has evaporated. Stir in the spinach and cook for 1 minute until it wilts, then season to taste with salt and pepper.

4. Wrap the naan breads in a piece of kitchen foil and warm them in the oven for 5 minutes.

5. Spread the warm naans with the mango mayo, then sprinkle them with a little shredded lettuce. Top with the jackfruit filling, sliced red onion and coriander. Add a spoonful of yoghurt and fold the naan over to enclose the filling. Serve immediately.

TIP For a super-quick mango mayo, stir some mango chutney into the vegan mayo.

VEGAN TLT SANDWICH

**SERVES 4
PREP: 15 MINUTES
COOK: 4-8 MINUTES**

400g/14oz extra-firm tofu

2 tbsp cornflour (cornstarch)

2 tbsp sunflower oil

8 slices wholegrain, wholemeal or multi-seed bread

4 tbsp Vegan mayonnaise (see page 13)

1 ripe avocado, peeled, stoned (pitted) and mashed

2 ripe tomatoes, sliced

sriracha sauce, for drizzling

a few crisp cos (romaine) or iceberg lettuce leaves, shredded

salt and freshly ground black pepper

VARIATIONS

- Marinate the tofu before frying for additional flavour.
- You can use any hot sauce, e.g. sweet Thai chilli or Tabasco.
- Add some roasted vegetables.
- Add some vegan 'bacon'.

EVERYONE'S HEARD OF THE BLT SANDWICH BUT HOW ABOUT THIS DELICIOUS VEGAN VERSION – THE TLT? IT'S MADE WITH CRISPY FRIED TOFU (INSTEAD OF BACON), LETTUCE, TOMATO, CREAMY AVOCADO AND VEGAN MAYONNAISE.

1. Cut the tofu into slices and dust them lightly with cornflour. Season with a little salt and pepper.
2. Heat the oil in a frying pan (skillet) set over a medium heat and cook the tofu, in batches (do not overcrowd the pan), for 1–2 minutes on each side until the slices are crisp and golden. Remove them with a slotted spoon and drain them on kitchen paper (paper towels).
3. Lightly toast the bread and spread 4 slices with the mashed avocado and the remaining slices with the mayonnaise.
4. Arrange the sliced tomatoes over the avocado and top with the hot fried tofu. Drizzle with the sriracha sauce and cover with the lettuce leaves. Top with the remaining toasted bread, spread with mayo.
5. Cut the sandwiches in half or quarters and serve immediately.

HALLOUMI SALAD WRAPS

SERVES 4
PREP: 20 MINUTES
COOK: 8-12 MINUTES

1 tbsp olive oil
500g/1lb 2oz halloumi, sliced
1 tsp dried oregano
4 large wraps or flatbreads
a few crisp lettuce leaves, e.g. cos
   (romaine), shredded
2 ripe tomatoes, coarsely chopped
1 small red onion, thinly sliced
sea salt and freshly ground
   black pepper
chopped fresh flat-leaf parsley,
   for sprinkling
smoked paprika, for dusting

TZATZIKI MAYO

175g/6oz (¾ cup) Greek yoghurt
50g/2oz (¼ cup) mayonnaise
¼ cucumber, diced
1 garlic clove, crushed
a few sprigs of mint, chopped
a few sprigs of dill, chopped
grated zest and juice of
   ½ small lemon

VARIATIONS

- Dust the halloumi slices with a
  little flour before cooking them
  to make them more crispy.
- Drizzle with hot sauce or
  pomegranate molasses.
- If you're really hungry, add
  some French fries to the wraps!

THESE VEGETARIAN WRAPS ARE FILLED WITH CRISP, GOLDEN FRIED HALLOUMI, SOME GREEK SALAD AND LEMONY TZATZIKI MAYO. IF YOU ARE SHORT OF TIME YOU CAN JUST MIX SOME GOOD-QUALITY MAYONNAISE INTO A TUB OF SUPERMARKET TZATZIKI!

1. Make the tzatziki mayo: mix all the ingredients together in a bowl. Season to taste with salt and pepper. Cover the bowl and chill the mayo in the fridge until required.
2. Heat the oil in a large frying pan (skillet) or ridged griddle pan set over a medium heat. Fry the halloumi slices in batches for 2–3 minutes on each side until they are crisp and golden and starting to soften inside. Remove and drain them on kitchen paper (paper towels). Sprinkle with the oregano.
3. Preheat the oven to 150°C/130°C fan/300°F/gas mark 2. Cover the wraps or flatbreads in a piece of foil and warm them for 10 minutes in the oven. Alternatively, heat them on a griddle pan over a low to medium heat for 45 seconds on each side.
4. Spread some of the tzatziki mayo over the wraps, almost to the edge of each one, and top that with the lettuce, tomatoes and onion. Pile the halloumi slices on top and season them to taste with salt and pepper. Sprinkle them with parsley and dust with smoked paprika.
5. Fold the wraps over the filling and roll them up in baking parchment or foil to hold the filling in place. Eat them immediately while they are still warm with the rest of the tzatziki mayo on the side.

NOTE Vegans can use a plant-based halloumi-style cheese and non-dairy yoghurt.

1 red (bell) pepper, deseeded
    and sliced
1 green or yellow (bell) pepper,
    deseeded and sliced
1 large red onion, cut into wedges
2 tbsp olive oil
1 tsp dried oregano
4 large wraps
a handful of crisp lettuce,
    e.g. cos (romaine), shredded
2 ripe tomatoes, sliced
85g/3oz feta cheese, crumbled
salt and freshly ground
    black pepper
lemon wedges, to serve

SPICY CHICKEN

1 small onion, cut into chunks
3 garlic cloves, crushed
½ tsp ground cumin
¼ tsp cayenne pepper
3 tbsp olive oil
450g/1lb chicken breast fillets,
    cut into bite-sized cubes

HARISSA YOGHURT MAYO

120ml/4fl oz (½ cup) Greek
    yoghurt
2 tablespoons mayonnaise
2 tbsp soured cream
a pinch of garlic powder
2–3 tsp harissa paste
a dash of lemon juice

SPICY CHICKEN GYROS

GYROS, WRAPPED IN FOIL OR PAPER FOR EASY HANDLING, ARE TRADITIONAL GREEK STREET FOOD.

1. Make the spicy chicken: blitz the onion, garlic, spices and oil in a blender or food processor. Spoon the mixture into a bowl, stir in the chicken and season with salt and pepper. Cover the bowl and chill it in the fridge for 30 minutes.
2. Next make the mayo: mix all the ingredients together in a bowl, adding the harissa a little at a time and tasting until it has enough heat for you. Cover the bowl and chill it in the fridge until required. It will stay fresh for up to 3 days.
3. Brush the pepper slices and onion wedges with olive oil, sprinkle them with oregano, and season with salt and pepper.
4. Set a ridged griddle pan over a medium to high heat and cook the vegetables in batches for 2–3 minutes on each side, or until they are just tender and attractively striped. Drain them on kitchen paper (paper towels) and keep them warm.
5. Meanwhile, preheat the grill (broiler) until it's very hot. Put the marinated chicken pieces in a grill pan lined with foil and grill them for 6–8 minutes, turning them occasionally, until they are thoroughly cooked. Remove them and keep them warm.
6. Warm the wraps on the hot griddle pan and place each one on a large square of foil or baking parchment. Divide the vegetables and chicken between them and top with the lettuce and tomatoes. Drizzle with the mayo and sprinkle with feta. Fold the wraps around the filling and roll them up tightly in the foil or baking parchment, folding in one end to stop the filling falling out of the bottom. Serve with lemon wedges for squeezing.

TIP Harissa paste is very fiery and powerful, so add it gradually and err on the safe side. People can always add more themselves if they want.

SERVES 4
PREP: 20 MINUTES
CHILL: 1 HOUR +
COOK: 8-12 MINUTES

MARYLAND CRAB CAKES

2 tbsp mayonnaise

1 medium free-range egg

2 tsp lemon juice

a splash of Worcestershire sauce

2 tsp Dijon mustard powder

500g/1lb 2oz white crabmeat

45g/1½oz saltines or cream
    crackers, crushed

2 tbsp chopped fresh parsley

clarified butter, for frying

sea salt and freshly ground
    black pepper

TARTARE SAUCE

4 tbsp mayonnaise

1 hard-boiled egg, peeled
    and chopped

3 gherkins, diced

1 tbsp diced capers

1 tbsp chopped fresh parsley

a squeeze of lemon juice

VARIATIONS

- Add a teaspoon of chopped dill
  or even some diced jalapeño
  chilli to the tartare sauce.
- Substitute powdered English
  mustard for the Dijon mustard.
- If you like spicy crab cakes, add
  more Worcestershire sauce or
  some Old Bay seasoning.

FOR THE BEST RESULTS, USE LUMP CRABMEAT RATHER THAN FLAKED TO GIVE THESE CRAB CAKES THEIR DISTINCTIVE TEXTURE. JUST CHECK THE CRABMEAT TO MAKE SURE THAT IT DOES NOT CONTAIN ANY SMALL PIECES OF SHELL.

1. Make the tartare sauce: put all the ingredients in a bowl and stir them gently until they are well combined. Set the bowl aside while you make the crab cakes.

2. In a bowl, beat together the mayonnaise, egg, lemon juice, Worcestershire sauce and mustard powder until they are well combined.

3. In another bowl, mix together the crabmeat and some of the crushed crackers in a bowl. If the mixture is too moist, keep adding cracker crumbs until they soak up any excess moisture. Season with salt and pepper and gently fold in the mayonnaise and egg mixture together with the parsley.

4. Divide the mixture into 8 equal-sized portions and shape each one into a patty. Flatten them slightly and transfer them to a tray. Cover them with cling film (plastic wrap) and chill them in the fridge for a minimum of 1 hour to firm up.

5. When you're ready to cook the crab cakes, heat the clarified butter in a large frying pan (skillet) set over a medium heat. Fry the crab cakes for 2–3 minutes until they are crisp and golden underneath, a few at a time so as not to overcrowd the pan. Turn them over carefully with a spatula and cook the other side.

6. Serve the crab cakes while they are piping hot with the tartare sauce.

TIP These crab cakes are fried in butter, but you could use oil instead or bake them in a preheated oven at 230°C/210°C fan/450°F/gas mark 8 for 12–15 minutes.

VEGAN CHEESY SLIDERS

SERVES 4
PREP: 15 MINUTES
COOK: 25-30 MINUTES

2 large sweet potatoes
4 large field or Portobello
    mushrooms
olive oil for drizzling
a pinch of paprika or cayenne
a handful of baby spinach leaves
1 large beefsteak tomato, cut into
    4 thick slices
4 slices vegan mozzarella (or
    other melting vegan cheese)
salt and freshly ground
    black pepper

SPICY VEGAN MAYO

115g/4oz (½ cup) Vegan
    mayonnaise (see page 13)
1 tbsp sriracha or gochujang
    (Korean chilli paste)
a squeeze of lemon juice

VARIATIONS

- Use thickly sliced aubergine
  (eggplant) instead of sweet
  potatoes.
- Use vegan halloumi or
  goat's cheese.

THESE HEALTHY SLIDERS ARE LOW IN FAT AND GLUTEN-FREE. THEY ARE VERY VERSATILE AND CAN BE SCALED DOWN TO MAKE SMALLER VERSIONS FOR PARTIES. THIS RECIPE SUGGESTS FILLING THEM WITH CHEESY VEGETABLES, BUT YOU COULD ALSO USE REFRIED BEANS, FALAFELS OR YOUR FAVOURITE VEGGIE BURGERS.

1. Preheat the oven to 200°C/180°C fan/400°F/gas mark 6.
2. Peel the sweet potatoes and cut each one crosswise into 4 thick circular slices. Arrange them on an oiled baking tray with the mushrooms (gill-side up). Drizzle them with plenty of olive oil, and sprinkle the paprika or cayenne over the sweet potatoes. Season the vegetables with salt and pepper and bake in the oven for 10 minutes.
3. Remove the baking tray from the oven and place a mushroom gill-side up on top of 4 of the sweet potato slices. Place some spinach leaves inside each mushroom and cover them with a slice each of tomato and mozzarella. Top them with the remaining slices of sweet potato and secure the stack with wooden cocktail sticks (toothpicks).
4. Bake in the oven for 15–20 minutes, or until the sweet potatoes are cooked and tender but not mushy, and the mozzarella has melted.
5. While the sliders are cooking, make the mayo: mix all the ingredients together in a bowl, adding lemon juice to taste.
6. Serve the sliders with the mayo and some crisp salad.

TIP Soak wooden cocktail sticks in water for 20–30 minutes before using to prevent them burning.

1 tsp olive oil, plus extra for grilling

1 onion, finely diced

500g/1lb 2oz minced (ground)
    beef (15% fat)

1 medium free-range egg, beaten

1 tsp Worcestershire sauce

a few sprigs of parsley,
    finely chopped

4 seeded burger buns

a few crisp lettuce leaves, shredded

1 large tomato, sliced

1 small red onion, thinly sliced

salt and freshly ground
    black pepper

SRIRACHA MAYO

115g/4oz (¼ cup) mayonnaise

2 tbsp sriracha hot sauce

VARIATIONS

- Serve with mustard, tomato
  ketchup or dill pickles.
- Flavour the beef with Dijon
  mustard or crushed garlic.
- Top each cooked burger with
  a slice of cheese and pop
  them under a hot grill (broiler)
  until it melts.
- Add some sliced avocado
  to the burger buns.

CLASSIC BURGERS

IF YOU'RE TRYING TO FIND THE ULTIMATE BURGER, LOOK NO FURTHER. THE SECRET TO SUCCESS LIES IN THE QUALITY OF THE BEEF YOU USE. DON'T CHOOSE LEAN MINCED STEAK - TASTY BURGERS NEED SOME FAT TO KEEP THEM MOIST AND JUICY. IF YOU CAN BUY MINCED CHUCK STEAK FROM YOUR BUTCHER (OR MINCE IT YOURSELF), THIS IS THE BEST OPTION. THIS RECIPE SUGGESTS SERVING THEM WITH SRIRACHA MAYO, BUT ANY SPICY, MUSTARDY OR KETCHUP MAYO WORKS WELL.

1. Heat the oil in a frying pan (skillet) set over a low heat. Cook the onion, stirring occasionally, for 6–8 minutes, or until it is softened and golden but not browned.
2. Put the minced beef in a bowl with the beaten egg, Worcestershire sauce and parsley. Mix them together well and then stir in the fried onion. Season with salt and pepper, then cover the bowl and chill it in the fridge for 1 hour.
3. Make the mayo: mix the mayonnaise and the sriracha sauce in a small bowl and set aside.
4. Divide the minced beef into 4 equal-sized portions and shape each into a burger (patty).
5. Cook the burgers on a lightly oiled griddle pan or over hot coals on a barbecue for 3–4 minutes on each side, depending on how well done you like them.
6. Split the burger buns in half and toast them lightly. Spread some mayo over the bases and top with the lettuce, tomato and red onion. Place the burgers on top and cover them with the seeded tops of the buns. Serve immediately.

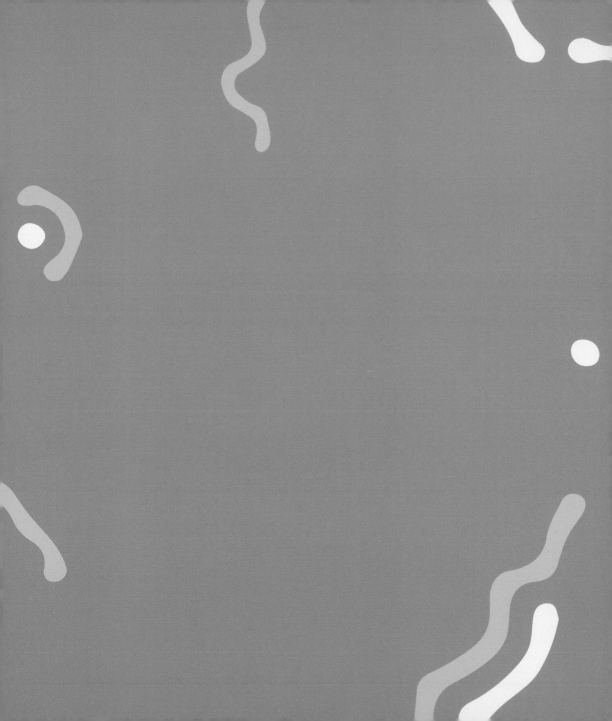

SALADS

AVOCADO GREEN GODDESS MAYO SALAD

SERVES 4
PREP: 15 MINUTES
COOK: 1-2 MINUTES

150g/5oz sugar snap (snow)
    peas, trimmed
1 cos (romaine) lettuce, trimmed,
    washed and thickly sliced
1 small cucumber, diced
4 spring onions (scallions)
    thinly sliced
1 large ripe avocado, peeled,
    stoned (pitted) and cubed
a few fresh chives, snipped

GREEN GODDESS MAYO

115g/4oz (½ cup) mayonnaise
120ml/4fl oz (½ cup) Greek yoghurt
a handful of flat-leaf parsley
a handful of basil leaves
a few sprigs of tarragon
1 garlic clove, crushed
2 anchovy fillets in oil, drained
juice of ½ lemon
salt and freshly ground
    black pepper

VARIATIONS

- Use mangetout instead of
  sugar snap peas.
- Add some sliced chicory
  (Belgian endive).
- Vary the herbs in the green
  goddess mayo: try fresh
  coriander (cilantro), dill
  or mint.

THIS CRISP GREEN SALAD IN A CREAMY GREEN DRESSING IS THE PERFECT ACCOMPANIMENT FOR GRIDDLED OR ROAST CHICKEN, BEEF FILLET, STEAKS, LAMB CHOPS, POACHED SALMON OR FRESH SHELLFISH. YOU CAN USE THE GREEN GODDESS MAYO AS A DIP OR FOR TOPPING BAKED POTATOES AND DRIZZLING OVER ROASTED VEGETABLES.

1. Make the mayo: blitz the mayonnaise, yoghurt, herbs, garlic, anchovies and lemon juice in a blender or food processor until they are smooth. Season to taste with salt and pepper, adding more lemon juice if needed.
2. Put the sugar snap peas into a saucepan of boiling salted water and boil them for 1–2 minutes, or until *al dente* (just tender but still crunchy). Drain them and set them aside to cool. Pat them dry with kitchen paper (paper towels).
3. In a large bowl, mix together the lettuce, cucumber, spring onions and avocado. Gently stir in the sugar snap peas and toss them lightly in the dressing. Check the seasoning and sprinkle with snipped chives.

NOTE Vegetarians can substitute 2 teaspoons of capers for the anchovies. For a vegan option, omit the anchovies and use Vegan mayo (see page 13) and cashew cream instead of yoghurt.

SERVES 4
PREP: 15 MINUTES
COOK: 30 MINUTES

1 red onion, chopped
2 garlic cloves, crushed
a pinch of chilli powder
1 tbsp cider vinegar
2 tbsp olive oil, plus extra
  for brushing
juice of 1 orange
8 chicken thighs, boned
sea salt and freshly ground
  black pepper

CURRIED POTATO SALAD

800g/1lb 12oz new potatoes
2 tbsp Thai green curry paste
8 tbsp mayonnaise
4 spring onions (scallions),
  thinly sliced
a handful of coriander
  (cilantro), chopped
juice of ½ lime

VARIATIONS

- Use chicken breast fillets
  instead of thighs.
- Add some crushed garlic
  to the potato salad.
- For a lighter salad, substitute
  Greek yoghurt for some of
  the mayonnaise.
- Serve the potato salad with
  grilled (broiled) large prawns
  (jumbo shrimp).

THAI CURRIED POTATO SALAD WITH GRIDDLED CHICKEN

SPICE UP A POTATO SALAD WITH SOME THAI FLAVOURS AND SERVE IT WITH DELICIOUS GRIDDLED MARINADED CHICKEN. YOU CAN ENJOY THIS SIMPLE MEAL AT ANY TIME OF THE YEAR.

1. Cook the potatoes in a pan of salted boiling water for 15–20 minutes, or until they are just tender but not mushy. Drain them well and set them aside to cool.
2. While the potatoes are boiling blitz the onion, garlic, chilli powder, vinegar, olive oil and orange juice in a food chopper or blender to make a marinade.
3. Flatten the chicken thighs with a meat mallet or rolling pin and place them in a shallow dish. Pour the marinade over the top to coat the chicken.
4. When the potatoes are cool enough to handle, cut them into thick slices or chunks and place them in a bowl.
5. Mix the curry paste in a bowl with the mayonnaise, spring onions and coriander. Add the lime juice and if it's too thick, add some more mayonnaise or some plain yoghurt to loosen it. Season to taste. Spoon the mayo over the warm potatoes and stir gently until they are coated.
6. Lightly brush a ridged griddle pan with oil and set it over a medium to high heat. When it's hot, add the chicken thighs and cook them for 5 minutes on each side, or until they are golden brown and cooked through.
7. Serve the chicken immediately with the curried potato salad and some green vegetables or salad leaves.

SERVES 4
PREP: 15 MINUTES
SOAK: 10 MINUTES
COOK: 2-4 MINUTES

115g/4oz (generous ½ cup) raisins
50g/2oz (½ cup) pine nuts
400g/14oz small broccoli florets
8 slices streaky bacon or pancetta
½ red onion, thinly sliced

YOGHURT MAYO DRESSING

225g/8oz (1 cup) Greek yoghurt
4 5 tbsp mayonnaise
1 garlic clove, crushed
1 tsp clear Greek thyme honey
a squeeze of lemon juice
sea salt and freshly ground
    black pepper

VARIATIONS

- Use toasted walnuts or almonds instead of pine nuts.
- Add some heat with a pinch of crushed red chilli flakes.
- Use apple cider vinegar instead of lemon juice in the dressing.

NOTE Vegans can use dairy-free yoghurt, vegan mayonnaise and plant-based bacon, and also substitute maple syrup for the honey.

VEGAN OPTION

BROCCOLI AND BACON SALAD

IF YOU'VE NEVER EATEN BROCCOLI FLORETS IN A SALAD BEFORE, NOW'S THE TIME TO TRY THEM. BLANCH THEM QUICKLY IN A PAN OF BOILING WATER TO TENDERIZE THEM BEFORE TOSSING THEM IN A SWEET, GARLICKY MAYO DRESSING.

1. Put the raisins in a bowl and pour boiling water over them. Leave them to soak for 10 minutes, or until they plump up. Drain them and then pat them dry with kitchen paper (paper towels).
2. Set a dry frying pan (skillet) over a medium to high heat and toast the pine nuts for 1–2 minutes, or until they are golden brown and aromatic, shaking the pan occasionally. Watch them carefully and remove them from the pan before they catch and burn. Set them aside to cool.
3. Make the mayo dressing: put the yoghurt, mayonnaise, garlic and honey in a bowl with a dash of lemon juice and stir well. Season to taste with salt and pepper, and add more lemon juice or honey, if needed.
4. Bring a large saucepan of water to the boil. Add the broccoli florets and blanch them for 1 minute. Drain them immediately and cool them under cold running water. Pat them dry with kitchen paper (paper towels) and set them aside.
5. Grill (broil) the bacon or pancetta until it is crisp and golden brown, or fry it in a dry frying pan.
6. Put the broccoli florets in a large bowl with the red onion slices, raisins and most of the pine nuts. Toss them gently in the dressing until everything is lightly coated. Sprinkle with the remaining pine nuts and crumble the bacon over the top.

GREEK BEETROOT AND DILL SALAD

SERVES 4-6
PREP: 15 MINUTES
COOK: 25-30 MINUTES

675g/1lb 8oz whole uncooked
  beetroot (beets), trimmed,
  peel on
225g/8oz (scant 1 cup) Greek
  yoghurt
115g/4oz (½ cup) mayonnaise
2 tbsp olive oil
2 tsp red wine vinegar
1 tsp sugar
1 garlic clove, crushed
grated zest and juice of
  1 small lemon
a handful of dill, finely chopped
115g/4oz feta cheese, crumbled
salt and freshly ground
  black pepper

VARIATIONS

- Instead of red wine vinegar, use white wine or apple cider vinegar.
- Add some chopped spring onions (scallions).
- Use orange zest and juice instead of lemon.
- Substitute golden beetroot for red.
- Sprinkle some toasted pine nuts over the salad.

SERVE THIS COLOURFUL SALAD WITH SOME WARM PITTA TRIANGLES OR FLATBREADS, OR AS PART OF A MEZZE SPREAD WITH OTHER SALADS AND DIPS. THIS GOES WELL WITH SMOKED SALMON OR TROUT.

1. Place the beetroot in a saucepan and cover them with cold water. Set the pan over a high heat and bring it to the boil. Boil the beetroot for 20–25 minutes, or until they are tender and the skin peels off easily when rubbed with your thumb. Drain and set them aside to cool.
2. When the beetroot is cool enough to handle, peel off the skins then cut into cubes.
3. In a bowl, mix together the yoghurt, mayonnaise, olive oil, vinegar, sugar, garlic and the lemon zest and juice, until they are well combined. Stir in most of the dill and season to taste with salt and pepper.
4. Gently stir in the beetroot then transfer everything to a serving bowl. Sprinkle with the remaining dill and crumble the feta over the top. Serve immediately.

TIP This salad will keep well in an airtight container in the fridge for up to 2 days.

½ green cabbage, shredded

½ small red cabbage, shredded

2 large carrots, cut into thin matchsticks

50g/2oz (½ cup) beansprouts

4 spring onions (scallions), thinly sliced diagonally

1 red bird's eye chilli, shredded (optional)

a handful of coriander (cilantro), chopped

a handful of mint, chopped

50g/2oz (½ cup) chopped peanuts

MAYO DRESSING

115g/4oz (½ cup) mayonnaise

60ml/2fl oz (¼ cup) thick, creamy coconut milk

1 tbsp clear honey or agave syrup

1 tbsp rice vinegar

2 tsp nam pla (Thai fish sauce) or soy sauce

juice of ½ lime

1 garlic clove, crushed

VARIATIONS

- Add some red (bell) pepper or mango cut into thin matchsticks.
- Use Greek yoghurt or soured cream to make a creamier dressing.

VEGAN OPTION

ASIAN COLESLAW

YOU CAN ENJOY THIS CRUNCHY COLESLAW ALL YEAR ROUND, BUT IT'S PARTICULARLY GOOD IN THE COLD WINTER MONTHS WHEN YOU YEARN FOR FRESH SALADS AND RAW VEGETABLES. THIS RECIPE ADDS SPICY THAI FLAVOURS TO THE CLASSIC CABBAGE, CARROT, ONION AND MAYO MIXTURE.

1. Make the dressing: mix all the ingredients in a bowl until they are well blended. Taste and adjust the ingredients, adding more honey if you have a sweet tooth or extra vinegar or lime juice if you like a hint of sharpness.
2. Put the cabbage, carrots, beansprouts, spring onions, chilli (if using) and most of the herbs into a large bowl. Toss everything gently in the mayo dressing.
3. Serve the coleslaw sprinkled with the peanuts and the remaining herbs. This will keep well in a sealed container in the fridge for 2–3 days.

NOTE For a vegan version, use vegan mayo.

SERVES 4
PREP: 15 MINUTES
COOK: 30 MINUTES

200g/7oz dried brown or
  green lentils
2 tbsp olive oil
1 red onion, diced
3 garlic cloves, crushed
2 medium carrots, diced
2 celery sticks, diced
a pinch of crushed red chilli flakes
16 baby plum tomatoes, halved
juice of 1 lemon
a handful of flat-leaf parsley,
  chopped
8 thin slices smoked salmon,
  rolled up
sea salt and freshly ground
  black pepper
lemon wedges, for squeezing

QUICK LEMON MAYO

115g/4oz (½ cup) mayonnaise
grated zest and juice of ½ lemon

VARIATIONS

- Cook the lentils in vegetable
  stock (broth) instead of water
  for extra flavour.
- Instead of parsley, use
  chopped dill or mint, or even
  fresh basil leaves.
- Add some crunchy, lightly
  cooked fine green beans or
  mangetout to the lentils.

VEGETARIAN OPTION

SMOKED SALMON AND LENTIL SALAD WITH LEMON MAYO

THIS LENTIL AND SQUASHED TOMATO SALAD IS BURSTING WITH LOVELY EARTHY FLAVOURS THAT COMPLEMENT THE SMOKED SALMON AND LEMON MAYO. IT'S BEST EATEN LUKEWARM OR AT ROOM TEMPERATURE.

1. Make the mayo: blend the mayonnaise with the lemon zest and juice. Taste and add more if you like it very lemony.
2. Put the lentils in a sieve and rinse them under cold running water then transfer them to a saucepan. Cover them with plenty of cold water and bring the pan to the boil. Reduce the heat and simmer gently for 15–20 minutes, or until the lentils are just tender but not mushy. Drain them in a colander, reserving a little of the cooking water.
3. Meanwhile, heat the oil in a large frying pan (skillet) over a low to medium heat. Cook the onion, garlic, carrot and celery, stirring occasionally, for 8–10 minutes, or until tender.
4. Add the chilli flakes and tomatoes and cook for 5 minutes more or until the tomatoes start to soften. Squash them with a spatula or the back of a wooden spoon to help them burst. Stir in the cooked lentils and cook everything gently for 10 more minutes until it is warmed through and tender. Add 1–2 tablespoons of the lentil cooking water to make the mixture creamy.
5. Season with salt and pepper to taste. Drizzle with lemon juice and stir in the parsley. Set the pan aside to cool a little.
6. Divide the lentil mixture between four serving plates and serve with the rolled-up smoked salmon and the lemon mayo, with lemon wedges for squeezing on the side.

NOTE Vegetarians can omit the salmon and serve the lentils topped with crumbled feta cheese.

SERVES 4
PREP: 15 MINUTES
COOK: 10–12 MINUTES

250g/9oz dried pasta, e.g. penne,
    fusilli, farfalle
olive oil, for drizzling
400g/14oz cooked chicken
    breast fillets, chopped
300g/10oz baby plum
    tomatoes, halved
4 spring onions (scallions),
    thinly sliced
a large handful of rocket (arugula)
fresh basil leaves, to garnish
sea salt and freshly ground
    black pepper

PESTO MAYO DRESSING

115g/4oz (½ cup) mayonnaise
115g/4oz (½ cup) Greek yoghurt
2 tbsp green pesto
1 garlic clove, crushed
a squeeze of lemon juice

VARIATIONS

- Add some cooked peas to
  the salad.
- Substitute cooked salmon or
  tinned tuna for the chicken.
- Stir in some diced avocado,
  or add mashed avocado
  to the pesto mayo.
- Substitute watercress for
  the rocket.

CHICKEN AND PASTA SALAD IN PESTO MAYO DRESSING

A PASTA SALAD IS EASY TO MAKE AND A GREAT WAY TO USE UP CHICKEN LEFT OVER FROM A SUNDAY ROAST. YOU CAN ADD VIRTUALLY ANY SALAD VEGETABLES AND TOSS THEM IN A CREAMY MAYO–BASED DRESSING. THIS RECIPE SUGGESTS AN ITALIAN–STYLE PESTO MAYO TO FLAVOUR A DELICIOUS FAMILY SUPPER.

1. Make the dressing: mix the mayonnaise and yoghurt in a bowl. Stir in the pesto and garlic and mix well until everything is smooth and amalgamated. Add a squeeze of lemon juice and check the seasoning. If the dressing is stiff, add a little more yoghurt or cream.
2. Cook the pasta in a large saucepan of salted boiling water according to the instructions on the packet. Drain it in a colander then refresh it under cold running water. Drain it again and tip it into a large bowl.
3. Drizzle the pasta with a little olive oil and toss it gently until it is lightly coated. Stir in the chicken, tomatoes, spring onions and rocket, distributing them evenly.
4. Add the dressing and toss everything gently together. Season to taste with salt and pepper.
5. Serve the pasta salad immediately, scattered with fresh basil leaves.

SERVES 3–4
PREP: 20 MINUTES
CHILL: 30 MINUTES

1 cos (romaine) lettuce or 2 baby
   gem lettuces, sliced
4 spring onions (scallions),
   thinly sliced
2 ripe avocados, peeled, stoned
   (pitted) and cubed
a few sprigs of basil, torn
juice of 1 lime
3–4 tbsp vinaigrette dressing
sea salt and freshly ground
   black pepper

CRAB MAYO

1 medium free-range egg yolk
2 tsp Dijon mustard
200ml/7fl oz (scant 1 cup)
   light olive oil
grated zest and juice of 1 lemon
450g/1lb (1 cup) white crabmeat

VARIATIONS

- Serve with some baby
  new potatoes.
- Vary the herbs in the salad
  – try fresh chives, flat-leaf
  parsley, tarragon or
  coriander (cilantro).
- Sprinkle the crab mayo with
  crushed chilli flakes, paprika
  or cayenne.

CRAB MAYO SALAD

YOU CAN SERVE THIS CLASSIC CRAB MAYO WITH A FRESH GREEN SALAD OR AS AN APPETIZER, SPREAD ON BRUSCHETTA OR CRISP MELBA TOAST.

1. Make the mayo: whisk the egg yolk and the mustard in a large bowl until they are well combined. Whisk in a drop of olive oil and keep whisking until it is amalgamated, then add another drop and whisk again until incorporated. Continue one drop at a time until the mayonnaise starts to emulsify and then add the oil in a thin, steady trickle, whisking continuously, until the mayonnaise is thick and creamy.
2. Whisk in the lemon zest and juice, and then fold in the crabmeat, distributing it through the mayonnaise. Season to taste with salt and pepper. Cover the bowl and chill it in the fridge for at least 30 minutes.
3. Put the lettuce, spring onions, avocado and basil in a salad bowl. Mix the lime juice into the vinaigrette and sprinkle it over the salad. Toss everything together and season with salt and pepper. Serve immediately with the crab mayo.

TIP If you're using fresh crabmeat, pick it over carefully and remove any small pieces of shell.

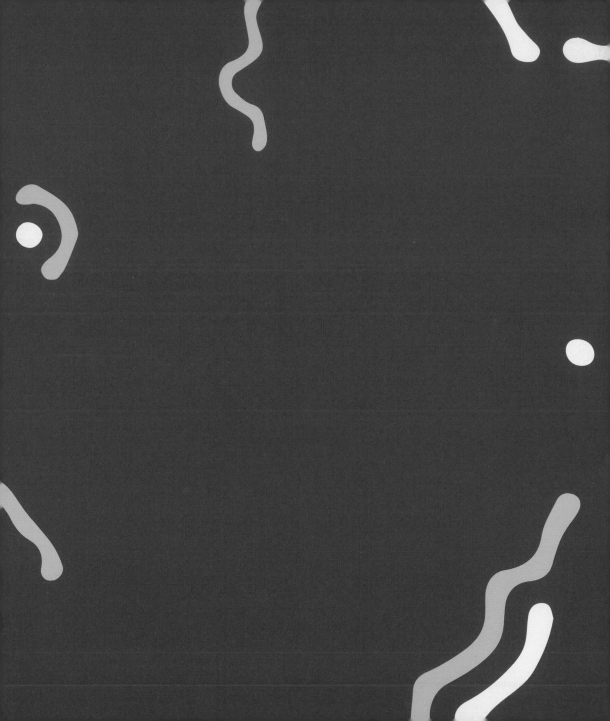

MAIN
MEALS

VEGETABLE TEMPURA

1 large aubergine (eggplant),
    thinly sliced
2 courgettes (zucchini),
    thinly sliced
1 fennel bulb, trimmed, outer
    leaves removed and thinly sliced
sunflower oil, for deep-frying
sea salt crystals, for sprinkling
lemon wedges, for squeezing

OUZO MAYO

225g/8oz (1 cup) mayonnaise
2 tbsp ouzo
a small handful of dill, chopped

BATTER

115g/4oz (1¼ cups) plain
    (all-purpose) flour
1 free-range medium egg
150ml/¼ pint (generous ½ cup)
    iced or cold water
1 tbsp olive oil
¼ tsp dried oregano

VARIATIONS

- Vary the vegetables – try
  sliced sweet potato, butternut
  squash, red (bell) peppers,
  mushrooms or broccoli florets.
- Serve with Wasabi mayo (see
  page 18) or Sriracha mayo
  (see page 18).

A GREEK–STYLE CREAMY MAYONNAISE PERFECTLY COMPLEMENTS THESE TENDER VEGETABLES LIGHTLY COATED IN A CRISP GOLDEN BATTER. THIS IS A GREAT MEAL FOR A WARM SUMMER'S DAY OR YOU CAN SERVE THE TEMPURA AS PARTY SNACKS AND CANAPÉS.

1. Make the mayo: put the mayonnaise in a bowl and stir in the ouzo and dill. Cover the bowl and chill it in the fridge until required.
2. Preheat the oven to 150°C/130°C fan/300°F/gas mark 2. Cover a baking tray with paper towels (kitchen paper).
3. Make the batter: using a hand-held electric whisk, quickly beat all the ingredients together in a bowl. Do not over-whisk – if the batter is smooth and lump-free it won't cling to the vegetables.
4. Heat the oil in a deep, heavy-based saucepan or deep-fat fryer until it reaches 190°C/375°F. Use a sugar thermometer to check the temperature or add a cube of bread to the hot oil – it's ready when the bread cube sizzles and turns brown in 30 seconds.
5. Dip some of the prepared vegetables into the batter, shaking off any excess. Use a slotted spoon or frying basket to lower them gently into the hot oil. Fry the vegetables in batches, taking care not to overfill the pan, for 2–3 minutes, or until they are golden and crisp. Remove them and place them on the lined baking tray to drain, then pop them into the oven to keep warm. Deep-fry the remaining vegetables in the same way.
6. Divide the vegetables between four serving plates and serve immediately, sprinkled with sea salt, with the mayo and some lemon wedges for squeezing. Serve with rice, pilaf or fried potatoes with a Greek salad, such as *horiatiki*.

TIP The ouzo mayo and batter can be prepared in advance.

VEGAN TACOS WITH CHIPOTLE MAYO

SERVES 4
PREP: 20 MINUTES
COOK: 15 MINUTES

3 tbsp olive oil

1 red onion, diced

2 garlic cloves, crushed

1 red chilli, diced

2 × 400g/14oz tins red kidney beans, rinsed and drained

4 tbsp hot tomato ketchup

4 spring onions (scallions), thinly sliced

8 baby plum tomatoes, diced

a small handful of coriander (cilantro), chopped

1 small cos (romaine) lettuce, shredded

8 taco shells, warmed

1 ripe avocado, peeled, stoned (pitted) and mashed

100g/3½oz (1 cup) grated vegan cheese

sea salt and freshly ground black pepper

lime wedges, to serve

CHIPOTLE MAYO

115g/4oz (½ cup) Vegan mayonnaise (see page 13)

1 garlic clove, crushed

1 tinned chipotle chilli in adobo, diced

½ tsp smoked paprika

2 tsp lime juice

THESE DELICIOUS VEGAN TACOS ARE FILLED WITH HOMEMADE REFRIED BEANS, WHICH TASTE SO MUCH BETTER THAN THE TINS YOU BUY IN THE SUPERMARKET. USE THE BEANS TO FILL WRAPS AND TORTILLAS OR AS A STUFFING FOR BURRITOS AND QUESADILLAS.

1. Make the chipotle mayo: put all the ingredients in a bowl and mix them well. Cover the bowl and chill it in the fridge until required.
2. Heat the olive oil in a frying pan (skillet) set over a low to medium heat and cook the onion, garlic and chilli, stirring occasionally, for 10 minutes, or until they are tender.
3. Stir in the beans and ketchup and heat them through gently. Season to taste with salt and pepper. Tip the mixture into a bowl and mash it coarsely with a potato masher. Stir in the spring onions, tomatoes and coriander.
4. Divide the lettuce and refried beans between the warm taco shells. Top with the mashed avocado, grated cheese and mayo. Serve immediately with lime wedges for squeezing.

TIP If you can't find chipotle in adobo in jars or tins, you can use chipotle chilli paste, which is available in most supermarkets.

NOTE Non-vegans can substitute grated Cheddar or Monterey Jack cheese.

SERVES 4
PREP: 20 MINUTES
COOK: 10 MINUTES

500g/1lb 2oz cleaned squid tubes,
    sliced into rings and tentacles
12 large prawns (jumbo shrimp),
    raw and unshelled
225g/8oz whitebait
vegetable or sunflower oil, for
    deep-frying
lemon wedges, for squeezing

LEMON MAYO

115g/4oz (½ cup) mayonnaise
grated zest and juice of ½ lemon

BATTER

115g/4oz (1 cup) plain (all-purpose)
    flour
1 tsp baking powder
2 free-range medium eggs, beaten
2 tbsp olive oil
300ml/10fl oz (1¼ cups)
    sparkling water
sea salt and freshly ground
    black pepper

VARIATIONS

- Use cubes of firm-fleshed
  white fish, mussels or scallops.
- Serve with Aioli (see page 17).
- Make a vegetable fritto misto
  with fennel bulb, artichoke
  hearts, courgettes (zucchini)
  and broccoli florets.

SEAFOOD FRITTO MISTO WITH LEMON MAYO

CRISPY DEEP-FRIED FISH AND SHELLFISH IS A POPULAR SUMMER DISH IN ITALY AND GREECE. A TANGY, SLIGHTLY BITTER, CREAMY LEMON MAYO IS THE PERFECT ACCOMPANIMENT. SERVE THIS WITH A CRISP GREEN SALAD OR A PLATTER OF FRAGRANT TOMATOES, DRESSED WITH FRESH BASIL AND AROMATIC OLIVE OIL.

1. Make the lemon mayo: blend the mayonnaise with the lemon zest and juice. Taste it and add more if you like it very lemony. Set it aside until required.
2. Make the batter: using a hand-held electric whisk, beat together the flour, baking powder, eggs and olive oil in a bowl. Beat in most of the water, adding more if needed, until you have a batter that is not too thick. Do not overwhisk – if the batter is too smooth and lump-free it won't cling to the fish.
3. Heat the oil in a deep, heavy-based saucepan or deep-fat fryer until it reaches 190°C/375°F. Use a sugar thermometer to check the temperature or drop a cube of bread into the hot oil – it's ready when the bread cube sizzles and turns brown in 25 seconds.
4. Dip the squid, prawns (shrimp) and whitebait in the batter, then put them into the pan. Deep-fry a few at a time so you don't overcrowd the pan. Cook them for 3-4 minutes until they are crisp and golden. Remove them with a slotted spoon and drain them on kitchen paper (paper towels). Keep the cooked seafood warm while you cook the rest.
5. Serve immediately, sprinkled with a little sea salt, with lemon wedges for squeezing and the mayo for dipping.

COURGETTE FRITTER BULGUR BOWL WITH FETA MAYO

**SERVES 4
PREP: 30 MINUTES
COOK: 30 MINUTES**

200g/7oz (generous 1 cup)
   dry bulgur wheat
240ml/8fl oz (1 cup) vegetable
   stock (broth)
½ red onion, diced
8 ripe baby plum tomatoes,
   halved
½ small ridged cucumber, diced
2 tbsp toasted pine nuts
a handful of mint, finely chopped
juice of 1 large lemon
3 tbsp olive oil
sea salt and freshly ground
   black pepper

FETA MAYO

60g/2oz (¼ cup) mayonnaise
60g/2oz (¼ cup) Greek yoghurt
1 garlic clove, crushed
75g/3oz feta cheese, crumbled
1 tsp dried dill (optional)

COURGETTE FRITTERS

2 large courgettes (zucchini)
1 onion, grated
1 garlic clove, crushed
a handful of mint or dill, chopped
4 tbsp grated Cheddar or
   Parmesan
grated zest of 1 lemon
2 free-range medium eggs, beaten
75g/3oz (¾ cup) plain (all-purpose)
   flour
olive oil for shallow-frying

THESE CRISP COURGETTE FRITTERS ARE SERVED WITH A CRUNCHY BULGUR WHEAT SALAD AND SOME SALTY FETA MAYO. DON'T BE PUT OFF BY ALL THE INGREDIENTS. IT'S QUITE SIMPLE TO MAKE AND THE MAYO AND FRITTER BATTER CAN BE PREPPED EARLIER.

1. Make the mayo: mix everything together in a bowl. Cover the bowl and chill it in the fridge until required.
2. Make the fritters: grate the courgettes coarsely, squeezing out any excess moisture with your hands. Place the grated courgette in a bowl with the onion, garlic, herbs, cheese and lemon zest. Stir in the beaten eggs and then fold in the flour. Season with salt and pepper and set aside.
3. Place the bulgur wheat and stock in a saucepan set over a high heat and bring it to the boil. Cover the pan and simmer gently for 5 minutes. Turn off the heat and leave it, covered, for 5 minutes, or until the bulgur wheat is tender and has absorbed the liquid. Transfer the bulgur wheat to a bowl and stir in the onion, tomatoes, cucumber, pine nuts, mint, lemon juice and olive oil. Season to taste.
4. Fry the fritters: heat the olive oil in a large frying pan (skillet) set over a medium heat. When it's hot, add 4–5 tablespoons of the courgette mixture (don't overcrowd the pan; the fritters will spread out as they cook). Cook the fritters for 2–3 minutes until they are golden brown underneath, then flip them over and cook the other side. Remove them with a slotted spoon and drain them on kitchen paper (paper towels). Keep them warm while you cook the rest of the mixture.
5. Divide the bulgur salad between four shallow serving bowls and place the hot fritters on top. Serve immediately with the mayo.

4 chicken breasts, skinned
and boned
plain (all-purpose) flour, for dusting
1 medium free-range egg, beaten
100g/3½oz (2 cups) panko
breadcrumbs
vegetable oil, for frying
boiled white rice, to serve
2 spring onions (scallions), thinly
sliced, to serve
a few sprigs of coriander (cilantro),
chopped, to serve

KATSU MAYO

4 tbsp mayonnaise
3 tbsp ketchup
1 tbsp soy sauce
1 tsp mirin
1 tsp Worcestershire sauce
1 tsp curry powder
1 tsp brown sugar or clear honey
1 tsp grated fresh root ginger
1 garlic clove, crushed
a dash of lime juice

VARIATIONS

- Use crushed cornflakes instead
  of panko crumbs.
- Serve sprinkled with black or
  white sesame seeds.

CHICKEN KATSU

CRISPY GOLDEN BROWN CHICKEN SERVED ON A BED OF RICE WITH A SPICY KATSU MAYO IS AN EASY WEEKNIGHT SUPPER. FOR A HEALTHIER OPTION, YOU CAN BAKE THE CHICKEN INSTEAD OF FRYING IT.

1. Place each chicken breast between two sheets of baking parchment or cling film (plastic wrap) and flatten them with a mallet or a rolling pin until they are about 5mm/¼in thick.
2. Lightly dust each breast with flour on both sides, then it dip quickly into the beaten egg and then into the breadcrumbs so it is completely coated. Place the coated breasts in a covered container and chill them in the fridge for 15–30 minutes.
3. Meanwhile, make the mayo: mix all the ingredients together in a bowl, then cover it and set it aside for 30 minutes to allow the flavours to mingle.
4. Heat the oil in a large frying pan (skillet) set over a medium to high heat. When it's very hot, fry the chicken breasts for 3–4 minutes on each side until they are cooked right through, golden brown and crisp. You may have to do this in batches. Drain the cooked breasts on kitchen paper (paper towels), then cut them into thin strips.
5. Divide the boiled rice between four plates or shallow bowls and sprinkle it with the spring onions. Arrange the sliced chicken katsu on top, sprinkle over the coriander and serve immediately with the mayo.

SERVES 4
PREP: 15 MINUTES
COOK: 15-20 MINUTES

spray olive oil
600g/1lb 5oz thick cod fillets,
    boned and skinned
plain (all-purpose) flour,
    for dusting
2 medium eggs, beaten
150g/5oz (3 cups) fresh
    white breadcrumbs
salt and freshly ground
    black pepper
lemon wedges, for serving

TARTARE SAUCE

4 tbsp mayonnaise
1 hard-boiled egg, peeled
    and chopped
3 gherkins, diced
1 tbsp chopped capers
1 tbsp chopped fresh parsley
a squeeze of lemon juice

VARIATIONS

- Mix some paprika (sweet or smoked) or cayenne into the breadcrumbs.
- Add some chopped fresh dill to the tartare sauce.
- Use panko breadcrumbs instead of fresh.
- Serve with Aioli (see page 17) or tomato ketchup.

CRISPY COD GOUJONS

THESE SUCCULENT CRISPY COD FINGERS ARE BAKED IN THE OVEN, MAKING THEM HEALTHIER THAN FRIED GOUJONS. YOU CAN USE ANY FIRM-FLESHED WHITE FISH, SUCH AS HADDOCK OR LEMON SOLE. SERVE THEM WITH GREEN BEANS, PEAS OR FRENCH FRIES.

1. Preheat the oven to 200°C/180°C fan/400°F/gas mark 6. Lightly oil a large baking tray.
2. Cut the cod fillets into thick strips and dust them lightly with flour seasoned with salt and pepper. Dip them into the beaten egg and then coat them on both sides with the breadcrumbs.
3. Arrange the coated fillets on the oiled baking tray and spray them lightly with oil. Bake in the oven for 15–20 minutes, or until the goujons are thoroughly cooked inside and golden and crisp on the outside.
4. Meanwhile, make the tartare sauce: put all the ingredients in a bowl and stir gently until everything is well combined.
5. Serve the cod goujons piping hot with the tartare sauce and some lemon wedges for squeezing.

SPANISH TORTILLA

SERVES 4-6
PREP: 15 MINUTES
STAND: 15 MINUTES
COOK: 25-30 MINUTES

1kg/2¼lb potatoes, peeled
olive oil, for frying
1 large onion, very thinly sliced
8 medium free-range eggs
    (at room temperature)
sea salt and freshly ground
    black pepper

ROASTED RED PEPPER AIOLI

2 roasted red (bell) peppers,
    deseeded and ribs removed
a handful of basil leaves
juice of ½ lemon
225g/8oz (1 cup) Aioli (see
    page 17)

VARIATIONS
- Add a good pinch of sweet
  or smoked paprika to the egg
  mixture or even some
  chopped parsley.
- Serve with tomatoes or a
  crisp green salad.

THE GREAT THING ABOUT A TORTILLA (SPANISH OMELETTE) IS THAT IT IS BEST EATEN AT ROOM TEMPERATURE, SO YOU CAN MAKE THIS IN ADVANCE TO SERVE LATER OR KEEP IT IN THE FRIDGE OVERNIGHT. IT'S GREAT FOR PACKED LUNCHES AND PICNICS, TOO.

1. Make the red pepper aioli: pulse the red pepper flesh and basil in a blender or food processor. Add the lemon juice and aioli and pulse until everything is well combined and smooth. Check the seasoning, transfer to a bowl, cover and chill until required.
2. Cut the potatoes into thin slices about 5mm/¼in thick. Pat the slices dry with kitchen paper (paper towels).
3. Pour olive oil into a large non-stick frying pan (skillet) 1cm/½in deep. Set the pan over a low to medium heat and when hot, add the potatoes. Cook them for 15–20 minutes, turning occasionally with a spatula, until tender and golden. Remove with a slotted spoon and drain on kitchen paper (paper towels). Discard the oil but don't wash the pan.
4. Meanwhile, fry the onion in a little oil, stirring occasionally, in another frying pan set over a low heat, for 15–20 minutes, or until tender, golden and starting to caramelize.
5. Beat the eggs in a large bowl, then stir in the onions and potatoes. Season and set aside for 15 minutes.
6. Set the potato pan over a low heat, adding a little oil. Pour in the egg mixture and cook gently for 5–6 minutes, or until the tortilla is set and golden brown underneath. Carefully and gently, flip the tortilla over to cook the other side – you can use a large plate to help you. Cook until set and golden underneath, then slide it onto a wooden board.
7. Cut the tortilla into wedges and serve with the roasted red pepper aioli.

TIP For the best results, use waxy potatoes, e.g. Maris Piper, to make the tortilla.

750ml/1¼ pints (generous 3 cups) water
120ml/4fl oz (½ cup) white wine
1 onion, quartered
1 carrot, cubed
2 celery sticks, diced
a few sprigs of thyme and sage
2 bay leaves
1 tsp black peppercorns
1 tsp sea salt
1kg/2lb 2oz lean rose veal rump
capers and lemon slices, to serve

TONNATO MAYO SAUCE

115g/4oz tin or jar of tuna in olive oil
2 anchovy fillets
50g/2oz (¼ cup) mayonnaise
60ml/2fl oz (¼ cup) olive oil
juice of ½ lemon
1 garlic clove, crushed
2 tsp capers

VARIATIONS

- Add some chopped fresh tarragon or parsley to the tonnato mayo.
- Eat the tonnato mayo as a dip with raw vegetables.
- Pour it over thinly sliced sweet tomatoes and garnish with fresh basil.

VITELLO TONNATO

SERVING VEAL WITH A CREAMY FISH MAYONNAISE SAUCE SOUNDS AN UNUSUAL COMBINATION, BUT THIS CLASSIC ITALIAN DISH IS DELICIOUS AND WELL WORTH TRYING. IF YOU'RE IN A HURRY, BUY SOME SLICED COOKED VEAL TO SERVE WITH THE SAUCE - OR YOU COULD POUR IT OVER SLICED COLD CHICKEN OR TURKEY BREAST.

1. Put the water, white wine, onion, carrot, celery, herbs, peppercorns and salt in a large saucepan and set it over a high heat. When it comes to the boil, add the veal to the pan. Bring it back to the boil and then reduce the heat to a bare simmer. Skim any foam off the top, cover the pan and cook the veal gently for 1 hour.
2. Meanwhile make the sauce: blitz all the ingredients in a blender or food processor until they are well combined and smooth. The sauce should have the consistency of cream. To make it glossy, add 1 teaspoon of ice-cold water and pulse quickly. Check the seasoning, adding more lemon, salt or pepper as required. Transfer the sauce to a bowl, then cover and chill it in the fridge for at least 1 hour.
3. Allow the veal to cool in the poaching liquid, then remove it from the pan and carve it into thin slices. Arrange the slices on a large serving platter and spoon the sauce over the top. Serve, sprinkled with capers, with the lemon slices.

TIP For the best-flavoured sauce, you need to use high-quality tuna packed in olive oil.

NOTE The tonnato mayo sauce can be stored in a covered container in the fridge for up to 3 days.

SEAFOOD NOODLE BOWL WITH SRIRACHA MAYO

SERVES 4
PREP: 20 MINUTES
COOK: 2-4 MINUTES

175g/6oz vermicelli rice noodles

2 tbsp groundnut (peanut) or vegetable oil

16 large raw prawns (jumbo shrimp), shelled, but tail on

1 ripe avocado, peeled, stoned (pitted) and cubed

4 spring onions (scallions), thinly sliced

1 juicy orange, peeled, sliced and cut into chunks

a small handful of coriander (cilantro), chopped

sesame seeds, for sprinkling

salt and freshly ground black pepper

SRIRACHA MAYO

115g/4oz (½ cup) mayonnaise

1–2 tbsp sriracha sauce (according to taste)

DRESSING

2 tbsp sesame oil

2 tsp light soy sauce

juice of 2 limes

2 tsp palm sugar

1 red bird's eye chilli, diced (optional)

THIS SIMPLE, CITRUSSY RICE NOODLE SALAD MAKES A REFRESHING AND DELICIOUS MEAL AT ANY TIME OF YEAR. IT LOOKS REALLY COLOURFUL AND NEVER FAILS TO PLEASE. IF YOU DON'T HAVE RAW PRAWNS, YOU CAN USE READY-COOKED ONES WHICH WILL BE FIRMER AND LESS SUCCULENT.

1. Make the mayo: mix the mayonnaise and sriracha together in a bowl then season to taste with a little salt. Cover the bowl and chill it in the fridge until required.
2. Put the rice noodles in a large bowl and pour a kettle of boiling water over them. Stir gently to prevent the noodles sticking together and set them aside for 3–4 minutes (or follow the packet instructions). Drain the noodles in a sieve or colander and transfer them to a clean bowl.
3. Mix all the dressing ingredients together and pour the dressing over the rice noodles. Toss gently until the noodles are lightly coated.
4. Heat the oil in a large frying pan (skillet) set over a medium heat. Put the prawns into the hot pan and cook them for 1–2 minutes on each side until they turn pink and are cooked through. Do not overcook them or they will become tough and lose their juiciness. Remove the prawns from the pan and add them to the noodles.
5. Stir the avocado, spring onions, orange and coriander into the noodles, and toss everything together. Season to taste with salt and pepper.
6. Divide the noodles between four serving bowls and sprinkle them with sesame seeds. Serve immediately with the mayo.

NOTE Vegetarians can substitute crispy fried tofu for the prawns.

BOUILLABAISSE

4 tbsp olive oil

1 large onion, diced

2 carrots, diced

2 celery sticks, diced

1 fennel bulb, trimmed and diced

2 potatoes, diced

3 garlic cloves, crushed

750ml/1¼ pints (generous 3 cups)
good-quality fish stock (broth)

180ml/6fl oz (¾ cup) dry white wine

400g/14oz (2 cups) fresh or tinned
chopped tomatoes

a few saffron strands

500g/1lb 2oz fish, e.g. monkfish,
cod, red mullet, sea bass,
grouper, scaled, gutted, boned,
skinned and cut into large chunks

500g/1lb 2oz shellfish, e.g. lobster,
mussels, clams, large prawns
(jumbo shrimp), cleaned and
prepared

2 tbsp Pernod

a squeeze of lemon juice

a handful of parsley, chopped

sea salt and freshly ground black
pepper

garlic croûtons, to serve

QUICK ROUILLE

115g/4oz (½ cup) mayonnaise

2 garlic cloves, crushed

2 roasted red (bell) peppers,
skinned, deseeded and diced

a pinch of saffron threads

THERE ARE MANY RECIPES FOR THIS ULTIMATE FISH SOUP - THE SIGNATURE DISH OF MARSEILLES ON FRANCE'S MEDITERRANEAN COAST. YOU CAN USE A VARIETY OF VEGETABLES, FISH AND SHELLFISH AS WELL AS DIFFERENT FLAVOURINGS, DEPENDING ON WHAT'S AVAILABLE AND YOUR PREFERENCES. TO MAKE THIS QUICKER AND EASIER TO COOK, ASK THE FISHMONGER TO CLEAN AND PREPARE THE FISH AND SHELLFISH.

1. Make the quick rouille: stir all the ingredients together in a bowl or pulse them in a blender until they are well combined. Cover the bowl and chill it in the fridge until required.

2. Heat the oil in a large saucepan and set over a low to medium heat. Cook the onion, carrots, celery, fennel, potato and garlic, stirring occasionally, for 8–10 minutes, or until they are tender but not coloured.

3. Pour in the stock, wine, tomatoes and saffron. Increase the heat and bring the liquid to the boil, then reduce the heat and simmer gently for 20 minutes, or until the vegetables have softened and the soup has thickened a little.

4. Add the prepared fish and shellfish to the soup and cook for 5 minutes, or until cooked through and tender. Add the Pernod, a squeeze of lemon juice and the parsley. Check the seasoning, adding salt and pepper to taste.

5. Ladle into bowls, distributing the fish and shellfish evenly between them, and serve with garlic croûtons (see below) topped with rouille.

TIP To make the garlic croûtons, cut a baguette (French stick) into thin slices and brush them lightly with olive oil, then rub them with a cut garlic clove. Spread out the slices on a baking tray and bake in a preheated oven at 200°C/180°C fan/400°F/ gas mark 6 for 6–8 minutes until they are crisp and golden.

SERVES 4
PREP: 15 MINUTES
COOK: 1 MINUTE MAX
PER CUBE

800g/1lb 12oz lean rump,
   sirloin or fillet steak
vegetable oil, for frying
sea salt and freshly ground
   black pepper
Blue cheese mayo (see
   page 44)
Srlracha mayo (see page 18)
Dijonnaise (see page 16)
Cornichons (mini gherkins),
   salad, crusty bread and
   French fries, to serve

VARIATIONS

- Try serving with Katsu mayo
  (see page 86), Guacamole
  mayo dip (see page 24), Aioli
  (see page 17) or Horseradish or
  Wasabi mayo (see page 18).
- Use pork tenderloin or large
  prawns (jumbo shrimp)
  instead of steak.

BURGUNDY BEEF FONDUE

BEEF FONDUE IS A GREAT DISH FOR A CASUAL DINNER WHEN YOU'RE ENTERTAINING FAMILY AND FRIENDS. EVERYONE ENJOYS COOKING THEIR OWN CUBES OF STEAK AND DIPPING THEM INTO THE DELICIOUS TRIO OF MAYO DIPS. YOU WILL NEED A FONDUE SET (A TABLETOP FONDUE BURNER PAN AND LONG-HANDLED FONDUE FORKS). IF IT COMES ON A REVOLVING LAZY SUSAN SO MUCH THE BETTER - GUESTS CAN SPIN IT TO ACCESS THE DIPS THEY LIKE.

1. Remove and discard any visible fat on the steak and cut the meat into large bite-sized cubes. Lightly season the cubes with salt and pepper and divide them between four small bowls.
2. Lay the table with the fondue burner in the middle, together with the prepared mayo dips in bowls. Place a bowl of seasoned steak next to each place setting.
3. Half-fill the fondue pan with oil and set it over a high heat on the hob. Use a cooking thermometer to check the temperature and when it reaches 190°C/375°F, you're ready to start cooking the steak cubes.
4. Carefully light the fondue burner according to the instructions and place the pan of hot oil over it. Guests skewer a piece of steak on a fondue fork and dip it into the hot oil until it is cooked to their liking. Allow about 20 seconds per cube for rare; 35 seconds for medium; and 1 minute for well done.
5. Serve the cooked steak with the mayo dips, some cornichons, a big bowl of salad, crusty bread and some crispy golden French fries.

TIP If you don't have a thermometer to test the temperature of the hot oil, drop a cube of bread into the pan – the oil is ready when a cube sizzles and turns brown in 30 seconds.

95

BAKES & BRUNCHES

CHOC CHIP BANANA BREAD

SERVES 10
PREP: 15 MINUTES
COOK: 1 HOUR

3 medium ripe bananas, mashed
100g/3½oz (½ cup) mayonnaise
1 medium free-range egg, beaten
175g/6oz (1½ cups) plain
    (all-purpose) flour
1 tsp bicarbonate of soda
    (baking soda)
a pinch of ground cinnamon
½ tsp salt
100g/3½oz (½ cup) caster
    (superfine) sugar
85g/3oz (generous ¼ cup) soft
    brown sugar
50g/2oz (½ cup) walnuts, chopped
85g/3oz (½ cup) dark (bittersweet)
    chocolate chips
butter, for serving

VARIATIONS

- Add a few drops of vanilla
  extract.
- For a citrussy flavour, add
  some grated orange zest and
  juice.
- Use dried apricots, cranberries
  or raisins instead of chocolate.
- Vary the nuts: try chopped
  pecans, almonds or hazelnuts.
- Instead of chocolate chips,
  swirl in some Nutella.

THIS MOIST BANANA BREAD IS GREAT FOR BREAKFAST OR BRUNCH, OR FOR SNACKING AT ANY TIME OF DAY. SERVE IT PLAIN, SPREAD WITH BUTTER OR CREAM CHEESE, OR EVEN DRIZZLED WITH HONEY OR MAPLE SYRUP.

1. Preheat the oven to 180°C/160°C fan/350°F/gas mark 4. Grease and line a 23 × 13cm/9 × 5in loaf tin (pan) with baking parchment.
2. Put the bananas, mayonnaise and beaten egg in a bowl and mix them well.
3. Sift in the flour, bicarbonate of soda and cinnamon and stir them into the banana mixture along with the salt and sugar. Gently fold in the walnuts and chocolate pieces, distributing them evenly through the mixture.
4. Spoon the mixture into the lined loaf tin and level the top. Bake it in the oven for 1 hour, or until it is well risen and a skewer inserted in the centre comes out clean. Start checking after 50 minutes to see if the loaf is cooked.
5. Leave the loaf to cool in the tin on a wire rack for 15–20 minutes before turning it out. When it is cold, serve cut into slices with butter.

TIP This will keep well wrapped in foil or in a sealed airtight container in a cool place or the fridge.

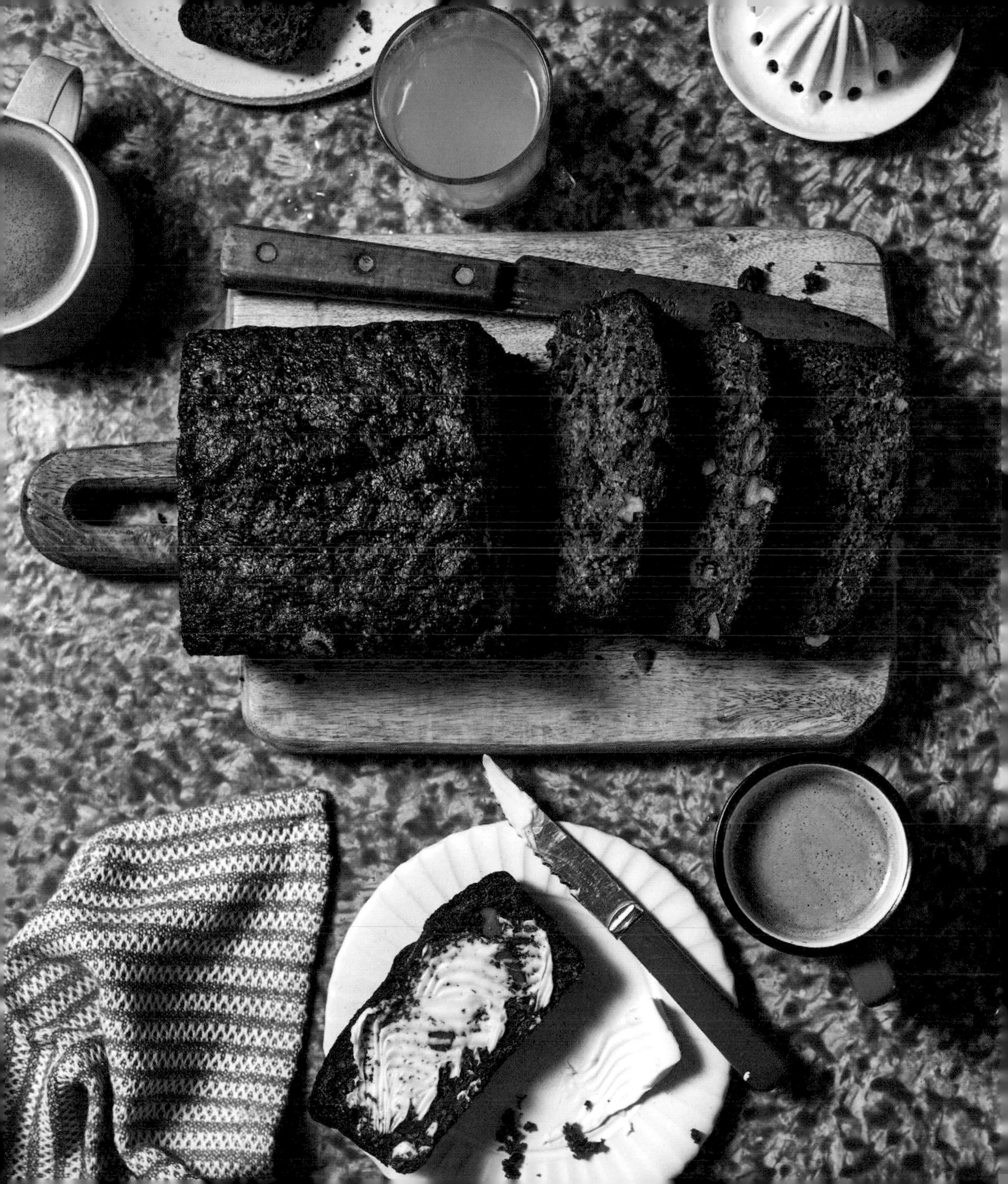

CHOCA MOCHA MAYONNAISE CAKE

**SERVES 8
PREP: 15 MINUTES
STAND: 5 MINUTES
COOK: 30-35 MINUTES**

50g/2oz (¼ cup) unsweetened cocoa powder

180ml/6fl oz (¾ cup) strong, hot brewed coffee

50g/2oz (1/3 cup) dark (bittersweet) chocolate chips

175g/6oz (¾ cup) mayonnaise

175g/6oz (¾ cup) caster (superfine) sugar

1 tsp vanilla extract

175g/6oz (1½ cups) plain (all-purpose) flour, plus extra for dusting

1 heaped tsp bicarbonate of soda (baking soda)

a good pinch of salt

icing (confectioner's) sugar, for dusting

raspberries and whipped cream or crème fraîche, to serve

VARIATIONS

- Drizzle the cake with chocolate or coffee glacé icing or a glaze.
- Top the cake with vanilla, chocolate, coffee or cream cheese frosting or buttercream and some chopped nuts.
- To make a plain chocolate cake use hot water instead of coffee.
- Serve with Greek yoghurt, mascarpone or even ice cream.

THIS MIGHT SOUND ODD BUT MAYONNAISE HAS BEEN USED AS A SUBSTITUTE FOR THE USUAL BUTTER AND EGGS IN CAKES SINCE THE EARLY TWENTIETH CENTURY. THIS RICH CHOCOLATE COFFEE CAKE IS VERY QUICK AND EASY TO MAKE AND DELICIOUSLY MOIST. EAT IT AS A TEATIME TREAT OR SERVE IT AS A DESSERT.

1. Preheat the oven to 180°C/160°C fan/350°F/gas mark 4. Butter or oil a round 23cm/9in cake tin (pan) and dust it lightly with flour.
2. Put the cocoa powder in a large bowl and pour the hot coffee over it. Stir in the chocolate chips, then set the bowl aside for 5 minutes. Beat the mixture with a hand-held electric whisk until it is smooth.
3. Beat in the mayonnaise, sugar and vanilla extract. Sift in the flour and bicarbonate of soda with the salt and whisk again until the mixture is lump-free.
4. Transfer the mixture to the cake tin, levelling the top with a spoon or palette knife. Bake the cake in the oven for 30–35 minutes, or until a thin skewer inserted in the centre comes out clean.
5. Leave the cake in the tin on a wire rack to cool and then turn it out and dust the top with icing (confectioner's) sugar. Serve slices with raspberries and cream. The cake will keep well in a covered airtight container for 3–4 days.

TIP You can use a deep 20cm/8in cake tin for a thicker cake but it will take longer to cook. Check it after 35 minutes.

BLUEBERRY MAYO MUFFINS

**MAKES 12 MUFFINS
PREP: 15 MINUTES
COOK: 20 MINUTES**

225g/8oz (2 cups) plain
   (all-purpose) flour
1 tsp baking powder
1 tsp bicarbonate of soda
   (baking soda)
¼ tsp salt
175g/6oz (¾ cup) caster
   (superfine) sugar
200g/7oz (1 cup) mayonnaise
1 medium free-range egg, beaten
120ml/4fl oz (½ cup) milk (dairy
   or plant-based)
1 tsp vanilla extract
175g/6oz (1½ cups) blueberries

VARIATIONS

- Substitute raspberries for the blueberries.
- Flavour with grated orange or lemon zest and juice.
- Serve the muffins with a large spoonful of Greek yoghurt.

EVERYONE LOVES BLUEBERRY MUFFINS, WHETHER FOR BREAKFAST, A MID-MORNING SNACK OR A TEATIME TREAT. THESE ARE SO MOIST AND PACKED WITH JUICY BERRIES THAT NOBODY WILL EVER GUESS THEY ARE MADE WITH MAYONNAISE.

1. Preheat the oven to 190°C/170°C fan/375°F/gas mark 5. Place 12 paper cases (muffin liners) in a 12-hole muffin pan.
2. Sift the flour, baking powder, bicarbonate of soda and salt into a bowl. Stir in the sugar.
3. In another bowl, beat together the mayonnaise, egg, milk and vanilla extract. Tip in the flour and sugar mixture and fold it in gently with a metal spoon in a figure of eight movement. Stir in the blueberries, distributing them evenly through the mixture.
4. Spoon the mixture into the paper cases and bake the muffins in the oven for 20 minutes, or until they have risen and are golden brown and the tops spring back when you press them lightly.
5. Cool the muffins on a wire rack. They will keep well wrapped in foil or in a sealed airtight container for 1–2 days at room temperature, or for up to 3 days in the fridge.

OATMEAL RAISIN COOKIES

**MAKES ABOUT 15 COOKIES
PREP: 15 MINUTES
COOK: 10-12 MINUTES**

200g/7oz (1 cup) soft brown sugar
150g/5oz (¾ cup) mayonnaise
1 large free-range egg, beaten
1 tsp vanilla extract
100g/3½oz (1 cup) plain
   (all-purpose) flour
½ tsp bicarbonate of soda
   (baking soda)
½ tsp salt
1 tsp ground cinnamon
a pinch of grated nutmeg
250g/9oz (3 cups) rolled oats
115g/4oz (¾ cup) raisins

VARIATIONS

- Add some chopped walnuts
  or pecans.
- Substitute dark (bittersweet)
  or white chocolate chips for
  the raisins.
- Use sultanas (golden raisins)
  or dried cranberries.

THESE SOFT AND CHEWY COOKIES ARE PACKED WITH HEALTHY OATS AND JUICY RAISINS. THE SECRET INGREDIENT THAT KEEPS THEM MOIST IS THE MAYONNAISE, WHICH REPLACES THE USUAL BUTTER.

1. Preheat the oven to 180°C/160°C fan/350°F/gas mark 4.
   Line 2 baking trays with baking parchment.
2. Use a hand-held electric whisk to beat together the sugar,
   mayonnaise, egg and vanilla extract until they are well
   combined.
3. Sift the flour, bicarbonate of soda and salt into the bowl
   and add the oats and spices. Stir well, then add the raisins,
   distributing them evenly through the mixture.
4. Scoop tablespoons of the mixture and drop them on to
   the lined baking trays, leaving 5cm/2in between them.
   Press down on them lightly with a spoon to flatten them
   a little. Bake the cookies in the oven for 10–12 minutes, or
   until they are cooked and golden with brown edges and a
   soft centre.
5. Leave the cookies to cool on the baking trays for 5 minutes
   and then transfer them to a wire rack and let them cool.
   When cold, store the cookies in an airtight container.
   They will keep well for 4–5 days.

AMERICAN BREAKFAST PANCAKES

SERVES 4
PREP: 10 MINUTES
COOK: 15 MINUTES

1 medium free-range egg

150ml/5fl oz (generous ½ cup) milk

½ tsp vanilla extract

2 tbsp mayonnaise

150g/5oz (scant 1½ cups) plain (all-purpose) flour

1 tsp baking powder

2 tbsp caster (superfine) sugar

vegetable oil, for greasing

maple syrup, for drizzling

berries, sliced banana, Greek yoghurt or crispy bacon, to serve

VARIATIONS

- Add some protein-rich chia seeds to the pancake batter.
- Stir in some blueberries before cooking the pancakes.
- Add a pinch of ground cinnamon.

ADDING MAYONNAISE TO A PANCAKE BATTER MAKES FLUFFIER AND THICKER BREAKFAST PANCAKES – THEY CAN BE UP TO 1CM/½IN THICK. SERVE THEM DRIZZLED WITH MAPLE SYRUP AND FRUIT AND YOGHURT, OR, FOR A SAVOURY FLAVOUR, SOME CRISPY BACON.

1. Beat together the egg, milk, vanilla and mayonnaise in a bowl.
2. Sift the flour and baking powder into the bowl and tip in the sugar. Beat again until everything is well combined and you have a smooth batter. Pour this into a measuring jug.
3. Heat a little of the oil in a small non-stick frying pan (skillet) set over a medium heat. Add a small ladleful of the batter and cook it for 1–2 minutes, or until the top of the pancake starts to bubble and it's golden brown and set underneath. Flip it over and cook the other side.
4. Remove the pancake from the pan and drain it on kitchen paper (paper towels) and keep it warm. Cook the rest of the pancakes in the same way.
5. Serve the hot pancakes drizzled with maple syrup and with fresh fruit and yoghurt or crispy bacon.

CORN FRITTERS WITH CHILLI MAYO

SERVES 4
PREP: 15 MINUTES
COOK: 12 MINUTES

225g/8oz (1 cup) tinned sweetcorn kernels, drained

115g/4oz (1 cup) self-raising (self-rising) flour

½ tsp smoked paprika

2 medium free-range eggs, separated

1–2 tbsp milk

1 fresh red chilli, deseeded and diced

2 spring onions (scallions), thinly sliced

a handful of coriander (cilantro), finely chopped

3 tbsp groundnut (peanut) oil

sea salt and freshly ground black pepper

lime wedges, for squeezing (optional)

CHILLI MAYO

115g/4oz (½ cup) mayonnaise

1 garlic clove, crushed

1 tsp chilli powder

juice of ½ small lime

VARIATIONS

- Serve with Guacamole mayo dip (see page 24).
- Instead of a fresh chilli, use ½ tsp chipotle chilli flakes in the fritters.

THESE HEALTHY CARIBBEAN-STYLE FRITTERS ARE SURPRISINGLY QUICK AND EASY TO MAKE. SERVE THEM AS A WEEKEND BRUNCH WITH FRIED PLANTAINS, CRISPY BACON AND EGGS.

1. Make the chilli mayo: mix all the ingredients together in a bowl. Add salt to taste. Cover the bowl and chill the mayo until required.
2. Put the sweetcorn into a small pan and cover it with cold water. Bring it to the boil and cook for 2 minutes. Drain well.
3. Sift the flour into a bowl and stir in the paprika, salt and pepper and make a well in the centre. In a separate bowl, whisk the egg yolks and milk and then beat in the seasoned flour until you have a stiff batter.
4. Beat the egg whites until they are stiff in a clean, dry bowl using a hand-held electric whisk. Fold them gently into the batter using a metal spoon in a figure-of-eight movement. Gently stir in the sweetcorn, chilli, spring onions and coriander, distributing them evenly through the mixture.
5. Heat the oil in a non-stick frying pan (skillet) set over a high heat. When it's hot, add small spoonfuls of the sweetcorn batter, flattening them a little with a spatula, and fry them in batches for about 2 minutes until they are golden brown underneath. Flip them over and cook for 2 more minutes, or until they are crisp and golden. Remove the fritters with a slotted spoon and drain them on kitchen paper (paper towels). Cook the remaining mixture in the same way.
5. Serve the corn fritters piping hot with the chilli mayo on the side and some lime wedges for squeezing.

SEEDY SCRAMBLED-EGG BREAKFAST WRAPS

SERVES 4
PREP: 15 MINUTES
COOK: 15 MINUTES

4 seeded tortilla wraps
2 tbsp olive oil
1 small red onion, diced
1 garlic clove, crushed
2 juicy tomatoes, roughly chopped
6 medium free-range eggs
2 tbsp chia seeds
a few sprigs of flat-leaf
   parsley, chopped
a handful of baby spinach leaves
sea salt and freshly ground
   black pepper

CREAMY AVOCADO MAYO

1 ripe avocado, peeled, stoned
   (pitted) and mashed
1 garlic clove, crushed
2 tsp lime juice
2 tbsp mayonnaise

VARIATIONS

- Drizzle some chilli sauce over
  the filling before rolling up
  the wraps.
- Substitute spring onions
  (scallions) for the red onion.
- Use fresh coriander (cilantro),
  chives or basil leaves instead
  of parsley.
- Serve with Guacamole mayo
  dip (see page 24).

WRAPS FILLED WITH SCRAMBLED EGGS ARE A HEALTHY OPTION FOR BREAKFAST OR BRUNCH. YOU CAN EVEN EAT THEM ON-THE-GO AS YOU WALK TO WORK OR COLLEGE. ADDING SOME CREAMY AVOCADO MAYO TRANSFORMS THEM INTO SOMETHING SPECIAL.

1. Make the mayo: mix all the ingredients together in a bowl, adding salt and pepper to taste. Cover the bowl and chill the mayo in the fridge while you make the filling for the wraps. Preheat the oven to 150°C/130°C fan/300°F/gas mark 2.
2. Wrap the tortillas in a piece of foil and heat them in the oven for 5 minutes, or until they are warmed through.
3. Meanwhile, heat the olive oil in a non-stick frying pan (skillet) and cook the red onion over a medium heat for 8–10 minutes until it is tender. Add the garlic and tomatoes and cook for 2–3 minutes more.
4. Beat the eggs with the chia seeds and parsley. Season them lightly with salt and pepper and pour them into the pan. Stir with a wooden spoon until the eggs start to scramble and set.
5. Spread each warm tortilla with the avocado mayo and scatter over the spinach leaves. Pile the scrambled egg mixture on top and roll up each wrap tightly or fold them over to make parcels. Eat immediately.

INDEX